TORCH BIBLE COMMENTARIES

General Editors

John Marsh and Alan Richardson

FOREWORD TO SERIES

The aim of this series of commentaries on books of the Bible is to provide the general reader with the soundest possible assistance in understanding the message of each book considered as a whole and as a part of the Bible.

The findings and views of modern critical scholarship on the text of the Bible have been taken fully into account; but we have asked the writers to remember that the Bible is more than a quarry for the practice of erudition; that it contains the message of the living God.

We hope that intelligent people of varying interests will find that these commentaries, while not ignoring the surface difficulties, are able to concentrate the mind on the essential gospel contained in the various books of the Bible.

THE ACTS OF THE APOSTLES

'*Nothing Can Stop the Gospel*'

R. R. WILLIAMS, D.D.
Bishop of Leicester

SCM PRESS LTD
BLOOMSBURY STREET LONDON

334 00010 6

First published 1953
Second impression 1956
Third impression 1959
First Cheap Edition 1965
Second impression 1969
Third impression 1972

© *SCM Press Ltd 1953*

Printed in Great Britain by
Fletcher & Son Ltd, Norwich

UXORI CARISSIMAE
IN ITINERE APOSTOLICO
MELITA ROMAM
ARDENTI CONVECTORI

CONTENTS

I

THE APOSTOLIC BAND COMPLETED AND THE HOLY SPIRIT GIVEN
1-1.40

vii

II

PROGRESS, DIFFICULTIES AND TRIUMPHS IN JERUSALEM
3-5

III

PROGRESS, DIFFICULTY AND TRIUMPH IN THE GREEK-SPEAKING SYNAGOGUES
6 and 7

IV

PROGRESS IN SAMARIA AND TOWARDS THE SOUTH
8

VIII

THE FIRST GREAT GENTILE MISSION
13, 14

IX

AGREEMENT ON THE TERMS OF GENTILE
ADMISSION   111
15.1-35

X

ANOTHER GREAT SWEEP FORWARD   119
15.36-20.38

PREFACE

I have enjoyed writing this Commentary on the Acts of the Apostles, and I hope that it may enable its readers to enjoy Acts more, and to see how it fits into its place in the New Testament Scriptures.

I have tried to carry out, in relation to Acts, the purpose of this series of Commentaries, as set out in the general preface. This is a little more difficult to do with Acts than with some other books. For one thing, as it is a book of history, set in a certain geographical environment, there are rather more historical and geographical allusions than in most biblical books. Many of these need to be understood, and in a book which is intended for schools and colleges, as well as for the general reader, it has proved necessary to explain them. I have tried to do so as concisely as possible. Another problem arises from the fact that 'the message of the book' is integrally related to the history itself. I have tried to avoid preaching little sermons on the material, and hope that I have enabled the material to speak for itself.

I hope readers will find two things in this Commentary not always to be found, even in larger works on Acts. The first is that the book is treated *as a whole*, being divided into twelve consecutive sections, each of which marks a stage in the outworking of the writer's plan for his book, and indeed, of God's Purpose for His Church. I have taken as the connecting theme the phrase 'Nothing can stop the gospel'. The second is a rather detailed comparison between St. Luke's Gospel and St. Luke's story of the Proclamation of the Gospel. I am convinced that the two works are symmetrical, and are meant to be seen as such. This is not just an interesting literary fact, but has a theological significance. It witnesses to the fact that Christ's Body, the Church, is called to follow closely in the steps of her Lord and Head, Jesus Christ.

R. R. WILLIAMS

St John's College,
  Durham.
    Easter, 1953

PREFACE
TO PAPERBACK EDITION

The production of this Commentary in a new paperback edition, after some twelve years, gives an opportunity to bring it up-to-date in certain respects.

The most obvious need was to include in the Bibliography a few books from the vast mass of literature that has appeared in English, French and German, during the last decade. Some idea of its scale can be gained by noticing that Prof. E. Haenchen, himself the author of a massive commentary on Acts, mentions that more than three hundred and fifty new books and essays on the subject appeared between the 1955 and the 1961 editions of his book! I do not claim to have read all of this new literature, but I became acquainted with a good deal of it in writing an essay 'Church History in Acts: is it reliable?' to be published in *History and Chronology in the New Testament*, (Theological Collections, Vol. VI), S.P.C.K., at about the same time as this new paperback edition.

In addition to re-writing the bibliography, I have added an Appendix, showing those places where I wanted to be allowed 'second thoughts', or where I thought readers should be allowed to see views other than my own. I strongly advise students to go through the list of new notes, and to put a mark against the relevant points in the main part of the book. Then, when they study the main text, they will have a warning that there is some 'stop press news' in the Appendix!

A few minor errors that had escaped earlier scrutinies have been corrected in the main part of the book.

In commenting on the first edition, Dr. Nathaniel Mick-
lem was kind enough to say that I had 'never pretended
that an open question was closed'. Looking over the problems twelve years later, I can only say that most of the
questions are now more open than ever! Scholars of un-
challengeable repute continue to range themselves on opposite sides on such matters as authorship, date, and purpose.
Slowly through the mist, however, the shape of the land-
scape begins to appear. The main features of this emerging
scene are (1) the more clearly recognized 'solidarity' between the Third Gospel and the Acts of the Apostles; (2)
the importance of this 'Lucan' picture of Christian origins
as one essential element in the total picture given by the
New Testament, an element integral to it, not alien from it;
(3) the fact that Acts, along with Luke's Gospel, has a real
theological content and texture. Whatever people may think
about the validity of this theological outlook, about its
adherence to, or its deviation from, the central message of
the New Testament, its existence is not to be doubted or
ignored.

When once the theological style and nature of Luke-Acts
is realized, private judgment steps in and 'places' it at
various points on the map of primitive Christian thought
and life. Some still bravely put it in the first period of
Christian writing, making it almost contemporary with the
events it records. At the other end of the scale, some remove
it to the middle of the second Christian century.

In spite of all that has been said, I want to keep it, in my
mental picture, as early as possible. However, I cannot but
admit that I am impressed by the new light that is being
thrown on the strongly theological nature of the book, something of which I included in the first edition of this Commentary. While in theory 'theology' could appear early in
the Christian story (*Galatians* could well be written by A.D.
50), the more one imagines 'Luke' writing a self-conscious
treatise, rather than a chronicle, the more likely it seems

that the book emerged when theology and history had converged into a single unitary concept. I can no more settle these questions now than I could twelve years ago; but I hope readers may be encouraged, rather than repelled, by the fact that both author and readers are still joint-adventurers, penetrating a little more deeply into the truth of God revealed in this story of our earliest ' Christian fathers '.

RONALD LEICESTER

Epiphany, 1965

BIBLIOGRAPHY (Revised 1965)

There is no shortage of books about Acts. Here is a selection from them, including several that have appeared since the first edition of this commentary was published in 1953. Those in this category are marked with an asterisk.

The Beginnings of Christianity, Foakes Jackson and Kirsopp Lake. Five large volumes. Macmillan, 1920-33. This encyclopaedic work contains almost everything that can be said about Acts from the literary and historical points of view. Vols. I and II, on background and criticism, are useful for the general reader. Vol. III on the text is for specialists; Vol. IV, the Commentary, is suitable for serious students; Vol. V, Additional Notes, is full of interesting, erudite information. (Vols. II, III, IV and V are now o.p.)

Commentaries based on the Greek Text
T. E. Page, Macmillan, 1886. A concise, scholarly work, very difficult to beat, but written before some modern questions, e.g. that of Aramaic sources, had become widely discussed.

F. F. Bruce, Tyndale Press, 1951. Scholarly and fairly all-embracing. A very valuable book. Conservative in its judgments on historical question.

Commentaries based on the English Text
R. B. Rackham, Methuen, 1901. Still a great stand-by.

A. W. F. Blunt, Clarendon Bible, 1923. A useful small work.

*C. S. C. Williams, A. & C. Black, 1957. A good, clear exposition based on an original translation from the Greek.

Commentaries based on the German Text
*E. Haenchen, *Die Apostelgeschichte,* Göttingen, Vandenhoeck & Ruprecht, 1956 (republished 1957 and 1959). A massive commentary, representative of newer attitudes to

Acts, based on an original, very literal, translation into German.

*Bo Reicke, *Glaube und Leben der Urgemeinde,* Zwingli Verlag, Zürich, 1957. An interesting treatment of Acts 1-7.

*H. Conzelmann, *Die Apostelgeschichte,* Tübingen, J. C. B. Mohr, 1963. (A German text printed, but virtually based on the Greek.)

Books about Acts, or about the period covered by Acts
The Acts of the Apostles. W. L. Knox, Cambridge University Press, 1948. (Its value greatly exceeds its size.)

The Apostolic Preaching and its Developments. C. H. Dodd, Hodder & Stoughton, 1936.

St. Paul, the Traveller and the Roman Citizen. W. M. Ramsay, Hodder & Stoughton, 1903. (Now o.p.)

Studies in the Acts of the Apostles. Martin Dibelius, English edition, SCM Press, 1956. (Collected essays from the pen of the great German N.T. scholar. Invaluable.)

The Sources of Acts. J. Dupont, Darton, Longman & Todd. English translation, 1964, following French edition, 1960.

The Theology of Saint Luke. H. Conzelmann, Faber, English edition, 1960, following German editions, 1953, 1957.

Luke the Historian in Recent Study. C. K. Barrett, Epworth Press, 1961.

The Theology of Acts. J. C. O'Neill, S.P.C.K., 1961.

Type and History in Acts. M. D. Goulder, S.P.C.K., 1964.

Three Crucial Decades. Floyd V. Filson, Epworth Press, 1964.

The Semitisms of Acts. M. Wilcox, O.U.P., 1965.

On the problem of the text itself
In addition to Vol. III of *Beginnings,* students should consult A. C. Clark, *The Acts of the Apostles,* Oxford University Press, 1933, and general handbooks on the text of the New Testament, e.g. Vincent Taylor, *The Text of the New Testament: A Short Introduction,* Macmillan, 1961.

MAP
The Journeys of Paul

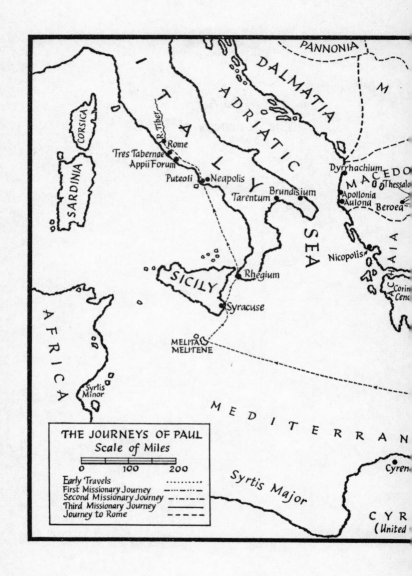

THE JOURNEYS OF PAUL
Scale of Miles

0   100   200

Early Travels ....
First Missionary Journey ....
Second Missionary Journey — · — ·
Third Missionary Journey ————
Journey to Rome — — — —

INTRODUCTION

WHO WROTE ACTS?

Acts is one of the books of the New Testament which is still ascribed by most modern scholars to the author to whom it was ascribed by second-century Christian writers, viz. Luke, St. Paul's travelling companion. We must examine the arguments which lie behind this very widely accepted view.

1. *The Gospel 'according to St. Luke' and Acts have the same author*

This assertion rests first on the obvious connection between the opening words of the two books. The gospel begins (Luke 1.1-4) with an introduction in which the writer addresses 'most excellent Theophilus' (otherwise unknown) and tells him that he writes so that Theophilus may know the sure foundation of those things in which he has been instructed. Acts begins (1.1-2) by referring to 'the former treatise' made by the author concerning all that Jesus began to do and teach, and this introduction, like the other, is addressed to Theophilus. We begin, therefore, with excellent grounds for assuming a common authorship. A close examination of the style and language of the two books supports this assumption. This matter is not quite as simple as some scholars have held, and there are some who do not consider that it points to this conclusion, but they are in a small minority. Among modern writers who accept it are Harnack, Ramsay and W. L. Knox, all careful scholars and acute critics. There are many words and phrases which occur only in Luke and Acts (i.e. not elsewhere in the New Testament), but which do occur in both books. There are sections in both books written in stylish Greek ('scholarship prose', as W. L. Knox has called it). Facts narrated only in the third gospel are assumed in the Acts (e.g. the reference to Herod's share in the trial of Jesus. See Luke 23.7-12 and Acts 4.27).

2. *The author of Acts was a companion of St. Paul*

Three considerable sections of Acts (16.10-17; 20.5–21.18; 27.1–28.16) are written in the first person plural, and hence are known as the 'we-sections'. There seem to be only three possible explanations of this fact. (*a*) They are a complete 'fake', inserted to give a quite false impression that the writer was an eyewitness. (*b*) They represent sections of a travel diary clumsily inserted by the author of Acts, though written by someone else. (*c*) They are the author's own travel diary, and he has used them for the part of his narrative to which they applied. (*a*) is a possible view, though one to which few will be attracted, unless forced to accept it owing to unavoidable difficulties in other views. (*b*) is really ruled out, as it is inconceivable that a writer of sufficient skill to produce the book would have left such clumsy alterations from 'they' to 'we', and *vice versa*. (*c*) is the view most widely held. We notice, too, that the 'we' sections have some special links between them, e.g. the first ends at Philippi and the second begins there. Did the original author of the diary stay there while St. Paul travelled around? But the 'we-sections' are integral to the rest of the book. Thus, e.g. Chapter 8 (*not* a we-section) is clearly assumed in Chapter 21.8 which comes inside such a section. Questions of style have been carefully considered, and the majority of scholars consider that the style of the we-sections is one with that of the rest of the book. We conclude, therefore, that the author of 'Luke-Acts' was actually a companion of St. Paul.

3. *Luke is the companion of St. Paul who most easily meets the requirements*

St. Paul gives at the end of some of his letters lists of the friends who were with him at the time. Those mentioned in Col. 4 are the friends who were with him at Rome, and as the last we-section takes us to Rome (28.16 'When we came to Rome') the list of friends in Colossians (written from Rome) needs special scrutiny. Some of the names are ruled out as they appear in the third person inside the we-sections (e.g. Aristarchus, Tychicus). Some of the other names might be considered, but here we have to consider the early tradition. Certainly by A.D. 170, and possibly much earlier, Luke was hailed as author of 'Luke' and Acts (see notes below). Until quite recent times the so-called medical language of Luke-Acts was brought in to support the con-clusion that the author was 'Luke the beloved physician' (of Col. 4.14), but it is now held that any cultivated man could have used the medical terms used in these books. It remains true, however, that the style is *compatible* with the view that the author was a physician.

4. *The evidence from the Second Century*

This is fairly weighty.

(a) A very early variant reading in Acts 20.13 is *thought* to have read, 'I Luke, and those with me, entered the ship'. If this conjecture is correct, the tradition can be traced back perhaps to A.D. 120.

(b) The so-called Muratorian Fragment, a list of accepted books dating from the last quarter of the first century, says: 'The Acts however of all the apostles are written in one book. Luke puts it shortly to the most excellent Theophilus, that the several things were done in his presence, as he also plainly shows by leaving out the passion of Peter and also the departure of Paul from the town on his journey to Spain.'

(c) An old prologue (about A.D. 170) to the third gospel says, after describing the gospel, ' And afterwards the same Luke wrote the Acts of the Apostles '.

The coincidence of the early tradition with the conclusions suggested by the internal evidence has been sufficient to keep most scholars faithful to the tradition. It must not, however, be assumed that the matter is absolutely definite. There are some real problems, of which the following are the chief:

(a) In Acts, St. Paul and St. Peter are represented as taking practically the same view about admitting Gentiles to the Church. In Galatians, their views, at least on one occasion, are seen to be in sharp conflict on a related question, viz. eating with such Gentiles after they have been admitted to the Church.

(b) Some writers think the author used a work of *Josephus*, a first-century Jewish historian who wrote about A.D. 93 (see below, p. 64). If he did, he must have been still alive sixty-three years after the Crucifixion, and it begins to get difficult to fit everything together. The author of the ' we-sections ' joined Paul at Philippi about A.D. 50. He would have to have been rather young to be still writing forty-three years afterwards.

(c) The traditional view rests on the assumption that we know the names of the possible authors, and only have to choose the most likely. It has to be remembered that our documents are few, and that they throw only a broken light upon the varied scene of first-century Christianity. There may have been several potential authors of Luke-Acts whose names we shall never know.

These points are mentioned to safeguard the reader from a hastily-acquired dogmatism on the Lucan authorship. It

is certainly the most probable hypothesis, and in this book
we shall not hesitate to call the writer 'Luke'.

5. *The author himself*

Assuming that the author was indeed Luke, what else do
we know about him?   Very little.   He was most probably a
Gentile, possibly from Antioch in Syria, or from Philippi
itself.   He could write excellent Greek, but often preferred
to write in the Hebraic Greek of the Septuagint (the Greek
Old Testament)—something in the same way as modern
prayers are often couched in biblical English. He saw
Christianity as a big, new, universal movement.   He had
wide and deep sympathies—especially for the poor, for
women, and for those despised as notorious sinners.   An
old tradition says that he died in Boeotia (Greece) at the age
of eighty-four.   He was, of course, a doctor, according to
Col. 4.14, but we must not think of him as holding a professional qualification like our own doctors.   According to
II Tim. 4.11, he was the only companion with St. Paul as
he awaited martyrdom at Rome.   All this information is
rather sketchy.   We shall never know much about Luke as
an historical personage.   He lives by his writings.   We shall
learn more of him by studying them than we should if a
papyrus sheet were suddenly dug up and found to contain
his *curriculum vitae*.

WHEN WAS IT WRITTEN?

Whole books have been written on the subject of the date
of Acts, and for the purpose of this book, only a brief treatment is necessary, or indeed possible.   Detailed evidence
(or 'alleged evidence') can be found in the larger works
listed at the beginning of this book.

When it is realized that reputable scholars, in modern
times, have given such widely different dates as A.D. 62 and

A.D. 150 for Acts, it will be seen that certainty is impossible.
The major points to be borne in mind in estimating the
probable time of publication are the following:

(1) It must have been written *after* St. Paul's arrival
in Rome, for that event is recorded in 28.16. (The
exact date of this arrival is uncertain, but it must have
been somewhere around A.D. 61.)

(2) It must be later than St. Luke's Gospel, as the writer
refers in Acts 1.1 to ' the former treatise ', meaning St.
Luke's Gospel. The gospel is usually dated after
A.D. 70 (the year of the fall of Jerusalem), as Luke
21.20 appears to modify Mark 13.14 in the light of the
events of A.D. 70, but this dating is itself now treated
as open to argument.

(3) If Luke used the *Antiquities* of Josephus, the Jewish
historian, Acts must be later than A.D. 93, the date of
Antiquities. On the question whether Luke did, or
did not, use Josephus (see Commentary on 5.36-37),
certainty is impossible.

(4) Acts was almost certainly written *before* the letters of
Ignatius, Bishop of Antioch (died A.D. 117), for his
letters contain a number of apparent reminiscences of
Acts.

(5) Acts was probably written *before* II Timothy, for
many scholars think the latter book—though written
in the name of Paul—assumes information only available in Acts. The date of II Timothy is uncertain, but
this letter also was almost certainly known by
Ignatius.

Points 4 and 5 compel a date earlier than, say, A.D. 100.
If Josephus was used, Acts must be after A.D. 93. Its date
then would lie between, say, A.D. 95 and 100. But if
Josephus was *not* used, and if the point about Luke 21.20 is
not considered decisive, Acts can be put back to A.D. 62,

and a very early date such as that is easier to support than a *moderately* early date like A.D. 80 or A.D. 70. For we can then explain the very curious point at which Luke stops his story. He stops it when Paul has been *two years* in Rome. Now this *can* be explained in terms of the purpose of Acts, which certainly involved the free proclamation of the gospel in the metropolitan city, and perhaps an interval like two years is necessary to show that this had really happened. But quite the easiest explanation is that Luke stopped his story at the point which events had reached, i.e. that he wrote before Paul's trial (or trials) and his subsequent martyrdom (say A.D. 64).

One further point is this. *If* Luke wrote Acts, and *if* he was, say, forty years old when Paul met him in A.D. 50, it would be convenient to get Acts written within the next twenty years or so. The later Acts is put, the harder it is to cling to the Lucan authorship. People did not always live to great ages in times gone by, and when they did, they did not always remain competent writers.

THE SOURCES AND RELIABILITY OF ACTS

Long arguments have taken place about the number and the nature of the sources used by Luke in the compilation of Acts. It is impossible here to enter into these arguments. All that is necessary is to set out those points which command general agreement, remembering that few, if any, of them can be taken as absolutely sure and beyond the range of discussion.

Among the principal sources probably used by Luke the following may be listed:

(a) Reminiscences preserved in the Church of Jerusalem
  For Acts 1–7 (for Acts 1–5.16 an Aramaic source

is thought to have been established); for 12; for
15.6-29.

(b) *Reminiscences of Paul*
Possibly for 6.9–7.60; almost certainly for 9.1-31; for
13.4–14.28; for 15.30-41; for 16.1-9; for 16.19-40;
Chs. 17, 18, 19, 20.1-4; 21.19–26.32; 28.17-31 (possibly
this last section comes from the reminiscences of the
Roman Church).

(c) *Reminiscences of the Church of Antioch*
For 11.22-30; 13.1-3; 15.1-5.

(d) *Reminiscences of Philip and the Caesarean Church*
For the whole of 8; possibly for 10–11.21.

(e) *Luke's own travel diary and recollections*
For 16.10-17; 20.5–21.18; 27.1–28.16.

Readers may be looking for some guidance as to how far
Acts is to be taken as historically reliable. A number of
points can be mentioned which encourage us to have faith
in its broad outlines, and in much of its detail.

(1) In Luke's Gospel we can see our author handling at
least one source of which we have knowledge, St. Mark's
Gospel. Though he handled it with freedom, interspersed
in it new material, and omitted that which did not suit his
purpose, what he did use he used faithfully, making only
minor corrections, mainly for literary or grammatical
reasons.

(2) Some of Luke's sources provided first-hand evidence
of the events recorded (see especially sources *b*, *d*, and *e*
above).

(3) Though not primarily a chronicler or an historian in
the modern sense, Luke had a sense for accuracy (see his
introduction to the gospel, Luke 1.1-4, and his chronological
notes, e.g. Luke 3.1-2).

(4) The speeches in Acts, though not to be taken as in
any sense 'dictaphonic' reports of what was said on each
occasion, are in fact remarkably suitable to their respective

audiences (e.g. Paul's speech to the pagans at Lystra, 14.15-17; his speech to the Areopagans at Athens, 17.22-31; that before Agrippa 26.2-23). Moreover, the speeches in the early chapters can be shown to harmonize closely with the gospel message of the primitive Church, as this appears in the Epistles of St. Paul.

(5) The 'local colour' in the references to political offices has been shown to reflect a high standard of accuracy in those places where it can be checked by modern archæological research (e.g. the deputy or pro-consul in Cyprus, 13.7; the rulers—politarchs—at Thessalonica, 17.6).

(6) The story of Acts enables us to weave together much of the fragmentary historical information to be found in the Epistles. If Acts is largely unreliable, it has to be admitted that we know very little about the course of *events* in the primitive Church (we should still know a lot about its *teaching*).

All these points lead us to take Acts seriously. But it must not be imagined that there are no difficulties. They may be listed, and can be taken as *caveats*, lest we should jump to wrong conclusions on the basis of the favourable points just enumerated.

(1) For much of his information Luke was dependent on traditions which had been in oral or written circulation for nearly thirty years. Probably there were few 'original disciples' like the Mnason of 21.16 from whom Luke could receive first-hand information about the early days.

(2) Some of Luke's chronological notes (in the gospel as well as in Acts) themselves raise difficulties (e.g. the taxing, i.e. the census of Luke 2.1-2 is awkward to fit in. Quirinius was Governor of Syria in A.D. 6, and then held a census, but if Jesus was born in the reign of Herod the Great, his birth must be dated about '6 B.C.'; again, Gamaliel in 5.36 refers to Theudas, whose rebellion, according to Josephus, had not yet taken place at the supposed date of Gamaliel's speech.)

(3) The pictures of Peter and Paul are assimilated to each other. Peter baptizes Gentiles and eats with them; Paul takes Jewish vows, and circumcises Timothy. Many think that this assimilation represents a re-writing of history, at a time when Peter and Paul had both suffered martyrdom in Rome under Nero, and when it seemed unfitting to perpetuate the differences of which we read in Galatians.

(4) There are many miracles in Acts, and these constitute a difficult historical question when we come to ask 'What actually happened?' In one case (that of the speaking with tongues at Pentecost) the interpretation given in Acts seems at variance with that provided by St. Paul in I Cor. 14. That strange and surprising events took place in the apostolic age is confirmed by the earliest evidence we have (e.g. I Cor. 12.10), but we have to remember that a pre-scientific age would not approach traditions of miraculous happenings with the caution, indeed suspicion, that is common in our day. They would not scrutinize evidence and insist on confirmatory witness in the way that we should. For further consideration of particular miracles, see the commentary, particularly on 2.1-13; 5.1-11; 5.17-42; 9.1-43; 16.25-40.

Altogether, then, we must say that Luke's work gives us invaluable information which we could ill spare; and that his general idea of primitive developments is coherent and convincing. But we must not expect the impossible from him, or judge him by standards quite inappropriate to his age.

THE THEME OF ACTS: 'NOTHING CAN STOP THE GOSPEL'

We now come to what is quite the most important part of these introductory sections. This concerns the purpose and nature of the book of Acts. What was it written for, and what is it all about? A right answer to this question will not only give us the necessary clue to the interpretation of many passages, but it will enable us to see what is the value and importance of the book for ourselves.

A two-volume work

It must always be remembered that Luke and Acts are two parts of one whole. Some have thought that they represent the first two volumes of a three-volume work, the last volume of which was either never written, or was lost at a very early stage. It is attractive to speculate on what such a third volume might have contained—the trial and final martyrdom of St. Paul, the arrival in Rome of St. Peter, and his martyrdom, the story of the Neronic persecution, and so on. But all this is speculation. What we actually have is *two* volumes, and it is as a two-volume work that we must consider Luke-Acts. Of course we are specially concerned with Acts, but it cannot be properly considered apart from its companion volume.

Now both these works are, as we have seen, addressed to Theophilus. He is otherwise unknown, but he may have been some important governor or other official in Rome of the Empire. (Festus is addressed by the same adjective, *kratiste*—noble, in 26.25.) Luke says that he wants him to know the 'sure foundation' of the things in which he had been instructed, so presumably Theophilus was a catechumen. He may conceivably, however, have been a friendly government official who had heard something about Christianity, and was prepared to go into it further, particularly perhaps to consider how it stood in relation to Judaism, which was an allowed religion. It seems quite clear that *one* of the purposes Acts had to serve was an apologetic one—it had to show that Christianity was the true successor to Judaism, that the opposition of the Jews was based on prejudice and factiousness, that sensible and wise rulers had nothing to fear from Christianity, and that those rulers who had been so foolish as to get involved in opposition to it had invariably regretted it. This, we may be sure, is one of the important themes of Acts. Peter and Paul may both get imprisoned, but they both escape! Festus, who would have set Paul at liberty, finds himself compelled to send him up to Caesar's court. The centurion who is charged with taking Paul as a prisoner to Rome ends with obeying his orders in the excitement of the shipwreck. All this was meant to impress Theophilus (and any other readers whom Luke had in mind) with the idea that behind Christianity was the unlimited power of God. Acts tells the story of Part II of a great drama, of which Luke is Part I.

A supernatural event in two stages

We see then that Luke is telling the story of a mighty event, and this event has two stages, both of which are supernatural. The gospel tells how God 'visited and redeemed his people' by sending His Son, Jesus Christ. The Acts tells how this event became 'a light to lighten the Gentiles' through the witness of the Spirit-filled Church. The stories run parallel to each other, and almost certainly Luke meant them to appear so.

The birth of Jesus in the gospel, through the overshadowing of Mary with the Holy Spirit, is paralleled in Acts by the birth of the Church through the gift of the Holy Spirit at Pentecost. The ministry of Jesus—healing and teaching—has its counterpart in the ministry of the Church which also consisted in healing and preaching. The passion of Jesus, solemnly prophesied and dramatically carried through, has a partial parallel in the persecutions to which the apostles are subjected, and particularly in the last journey of St. Paul to Jerusalem, in his arrest and trials, and in his terrible experiences in the shipwreck. It may even be held that the resurrection of Jesus has its counterpart in the

escape of St. Paul from the terrible storm, and in his safe
arrival and unhindered preaching in the mother city of the
Empire.

A good motto for both books, but especially for Acts
could be *'Nothing can stop the gospel'*. St. Luke shows
that the power of God was at work, first in the events connected with the life, death and resurrection of the Lord,
then in the proclamation of the Christian gospel, and in the
building up and extension of the Church.

The final word in the Acts is *akōlutōs*—without hindrance—and it is used to describe the conditions under
which St. Paul preached the Kingdom of God and taught
those things which concern the Lord Jesus Christ (28.31)
in Rome itself. At the beginning of Acts we read ' Ye shall
be witnesses unto me both in Jerusalem and in all Judaea,
and in Samaria, and unto the uttermost part of the earth'
(1.8). The whole of Acts is the story of how the preaching
at Rome emerged from the original commission, and how
every conceivable obstacle and difficulty was overcome.

Stages in the story of Acts

We are now ready to study more closely the successive
stages in the Acts story, and to see how they fit in to the
main scheme. The story can of course be divided and sub-
divided *ad infinitum*, but for our purpose we will divide it
into *twelve* stages, twelve at least having the advantage of
being an apostolic number!

1. The Apostolic Band completed and the Holy Spirit given (Chapters 1 and 2)

Matthias replaces Judas, and thus the apostolic band of
twelve members is complete once more. On this ' new
Israel', (the ' antitype' of the twelve patriarchs or tribes of
ancient Israel) the promised Spirit of power and of witness
descends. Not for nothing does the Spirit appear in the

form of cloven tongues, and manifest itself in the gift of tongues, for it is for *witness* that the Spirit is given. Very significantly, as soon as the Spirit is given, all the assembled company of Jews and proselytes hear the wonderful works of God.

2. *Progress, difficulties and triumphs in Jerusalem (Chapters 3-5)*

This section (which really begins at 2.41) describes the effective preaching of Peter and the other apostles, the healing miracles which authenticated their God-given mission, the various attempts of the authorities to restrain them, and the ignominious failure of these efforts. Internal corruption (as illustrated in the story of Ananias and Sapphira) proves as powerless to hold up the Church's work as does official opposition.

3. *Progress, difficulties and triumph in the Greek-speaking synagogues (Chapters 6 and 7)*

Ancient Judaism was divided into two halves, the Aramaic-speaking, 'Hebraic', Judaism of Jerusalem and Judaea, and the Greek-speaking liberal Judaism of the Mediterranean basin, that known as 'the Dispersion'. Now the second kind, though having as its *raison d'être* the maintenance of Judaism in the Greek-speaking cities, had also its special synagogues in Jerusalem (something in the same way as there are 'foreign churches' in London). It was to represent the interests of these Greek-speakers that the seven so-called deacons were appointed (see notes on 6). Now when there was a vigorous attempt to spread the gospel in these synagogues (6.7-10) there arose equally vigorous opposition, and Stephen, the chief of the new officers, lost his life. But this led to mighty victories. Saul was converted, though he was a witness at Stephen's death. Missions spread in all directions as a result of the very persecution (8.4; 11.19-21).

4. *Progress and difficulty in Samaria and towards the South*
   (*Chapter 8*)

Samaria stood in a kind of midway position between
orthodox Jewry and heathendom. Though of Jewish stock,
the Samaritans were not recognized by the Jews as being
proper Israelites. Their descent was marred by inter-
marriage with non-Jews. But Samaria was on the list for
evangelization (1.8). Philip, another of the seven, conducted
a mission there, and received the support and confirmation
of Peter and John for the work he had done. He also is
found evangelizing the Ethiopian Eunuch (8.26ff.), and as
the eunuch disappears towards Ethiopia we are left wonder-
ing whether he will found a church in the Court of Candace,
and like Naaman, set up an altar for Christ in the very midst
of the house of Rimmon!

5. *Saul, the Arch-enemy, is won for Christ* (*Chapter 9.1-31*)

This epoch-making event calls for little comment at this
stage. It is the supreme example of the truth that nothing
can stop the gospel! The chief persecutor is destined to
become the chief apostle.

6. *Peter as a missionary to Gentiles* (*Chapter 9.3–11.21*)

Two striking miracles are attributed to Peter, during a
mission to the coastal area in the West (9.32-43), but these
are only to prepare the way for an event of much more
significance. Through a divine vision, Peter (as we know
from Galatians not too strong an advocate of unrestricted
fellowship with Gentile converts) becomes the means whereby a Roman centurion, Cornelius and his household are
baptized and converted. That this event is very important
in Luke's scheme is clear from the fact that Luke tells and
retells the main events, making it *quite* clear that a mile-
stone has been reached. The point is that this is the first
case where *Gentiles* are given access to the Church and to
the gift of the Spirit (11.18).

A pendant to this story contains a very important piece of information. We refer to the account in 11.19-30 about the foundation of the church at Antioch, the capital of Syria. In this great Hellenistic city, as a result of the dispersion of Christians after Stephen's martyrdom, the gospel was preached to Gentiles in large numbers. 'A great number of them believed, and turned unto the Lord.' From this largely Gentile church there was soon to set out the first mission to Asia Minor, and later, to Europe.

7 Herod's vain effort to crush the Church (Chapter 12)

In Luke's Gospel, information was given about Herod Antipas's deceitful and equivocal attitude to Jesus. Our Lord called him 'that fox', and refused to satisfy him by working wonders when he was sent by Pilate to appear before him. Now we see Herod Antipas's nephew, Herod Agrippa I, a favourite of Rome, but almost equally a favourite with the Jews, trying to further his popularity by persecuting the Church. He puts James, the son of Zebedee, to death, and thinks that the execution of Peter would be equally acceptable to the Jewish people. But God steps in. Peter is delivered from prison by the miraculous intervention of an angel, and Herod dies a violent death as a result of sudden illness which strikes him at the very moment when the people are shouting, 'It is the voice of a god and not of a man' (12.22). 'But the word of God grew and multiplied.' No sudden disaster could interrupt the steady growth of the gospel and the Church.

8. The first great Gentile mission (Chapters 13-14)

The next two chapters are really vital. They describe the first missionary journey of Paul and Barnabas to Cyprus and mid-Asia Minor, i.e. to the cities of Galatia Province. The gospel is always given first to the Jews in their synagogues, but invariably they reject it, and at last Paul announces dramatically, 'lo, we turn to the Gentiles'

(13.46). This is an important turning point in Acts. From now on, interest centres in the Gentile mission, and the chief remaining interest in the Jerusalem church is in the question as to whether they will support and welcome the Gentile mission.

9. *Agreement on the terms of Gentile admission* (*Chapter 15.1-35*)

The question raised at the end of the last section soon came up for discussion in real earnest. (For the relation of this Jerusalem conference to Paul's previous visit to Jerusalem (11.30) and for the relation of both to Paul's words in Galatians 1 and 2, see notes on Acts 11.30 and on Acts 15.) Jewish emissaries came to Antioch, insisting that Gentile converts should be circumcised and keep the Jewish Law. This condition of entry might have frustrated the whole missionary movement. But it was not allowed to! 'It seemed good to the Holy Ghost, and to us,' wrote the apostles and elders, 'to lay upon you no other burden than these necessary things' (15.28), and they went on to outline some modest requirements in the way of concessions to Jewish custom in the matter of food. Once more the way had been opened for further advance.

10. *Another great sweep forward* (*Chapters 16-20*)

Paul, this time accompanied by Silas instead of Barnabas, sets out once more, and this time crosses over into Europe and founds churches at Philippi, Thessalonica, and Corinth, preaching also at Athens. After a short visit to Palestine, he conducts a long mission at Ephesus. He raises funds among the Gentiles for the Jewish church, to express the solidarity of the new people of God. At last he sets out for Jerusalem for the last time.

11. *Paul's Passion Narrative* (*Chapters 21-27*)

The journey to Jerusalem, Paul's arrest and frequent

trials, his terrible sea-voyage, ending with the shipwreck on Malta, are probably intended to form a symmetrical parallel to our Lord's journey to Jerusalem, His trials, death, and burial, in the gospel. The great speeches of Paul before the Jews, Felix, Festus, and Agrippa II are important expositions of Paul's (and Luke's) understanding of the gospel, and of God's intention that it shall be preached to all.

12. Victory! (Chapter 28)

In a strange and unexpected way, Paul finds himself at Rome. He is a prisoner, yet not by any means a defeated or condemned prisoner. In fact he is only there because he has exerted his right to be tried at Caesar's court (25.11). After a journey which only the Providence of God can be felt to have brought to a successful conclusion, Paul is allowed considerable liberty. He lives in his own house (28.30)—perhaps the word in the Greek means ' plied his own trade '—and preached with all confidence ' no man forbidding him '. Victory had been snatched out of apparent defeat. Resurrection had succeeded Passion. Paul had been united with his Lord, not indeed in actual physical death, but in every threat and appearance of it, not in actual resurrection, but in being the subject of a notable intervention by God, at a time when all seemed lost. That Luke is conscious of the many parallels between the stories of Christ and His apostles is, I think, the conclusion to which we are driven by much cumulative evidence. (For this, see the commentary, *passim*, on chapters 21-28.) It is not, of course, that Paul's escape and arrival at Rome are, in theological importance, in any way comparable to the Passion and Resurrection of Christ. It is true, however, that the *pattern* of failure followed by success, defeat followed by victory, weakness swallowed up in strength is considered by Luke to lie at the heart of God's dealing with men through the gospel.

The gospel had spread from Jerusalem, the centre of God's ancient Israel, to Rome, the centre of the political world, and the point from which it was to spread over Western Europe, and from which Augustine's famous mission to Kent was to set forth. Nothing had stopped—nothing could stop—the gospel. That was the message of Acts for its first readers, and that is its message for us to-day. The goal in Acts was but the starting point in the sixth century; the goal in the sixth century but the starting point in the nineteenth. Perhaps the goals of the nineteenth century, Africa, India and China will be the starting points in centuries yet to come. We can add chapters to the story, but Acts tells us how to interpret them. The recession now going on in China looks differently to the reader who has stood with Peter outside the prison-gates, and with Paul, before Agrippa, or among the startled Maltese on the shore on that stormy morning when Paul arrived there so unexpectedly. The exalted Christ still gives His Spirit to His Church, and in the Spirit's strength the Church can still proclaim its gospel, *akōlutōs*, none forbidding.

I

THE
APOSTOLIC BAND COMPLETED
AND THE HOLY SPIRIT GIVEN

THE ASCENDING CHRIST
COMMISSIONS HIS APOSTLES
1.1-14

The opening section of Acts serves as a bridge between the
Gospel of St. Luke and its sequel, Acts. After a brief reference to ‘the former treatise’ (1.1) Luke devotes the first
three verses of the chapter to a brief *résumé* of the events
of the forty days between the Resurrection and the Ascension. These days were marked by convincing proof of the
Resurrection, further teaching about the Kingdom of God,
and commandments to the Apostles (1.1-3). Vv. 4-14 go
into the story of the Ascension more fully. The *fact* of the
Ascension is assumed in many books of the New Testament
(John 20.7-11; Eph. 4.9-10; Heb. 1.3), but this is the only
narrative account of it. (Luke 24.51 involves difficult questions about the original wording used by Luke.)

It is difficult for us to realize the tremendous *theological*
importance of the Ascension in the apostolic age. It stands
for far more than a rounding-off of the story of the life of
Jesus, and His return to the pre-Incarnate state. Primarily
it meant the conferring on Him the supreme Lordship in,
and over, the whole Universe, a Lordship which in the Old
Testament had been felt to belong to God alone. Hence
the text most frequently used to interpret it was Psalm

110.1. 'Sit thou on my right hand, until I make thine enemies thy footstool.' To be 'at the right hand' of God meant to be associated directly and ultimately with Him in the government of the world. This is what St. Paul is speaking of in I Cor. 15.24-28. Other illuminating references to the doctrine are found in Rom. 8.34; Col. 2.15 (where the Cross, Resurrection and Ascension are thought of as an entity, as they are in Hebrews); Phil. 2.9-11 (one of the quite vital passages); and Eph. 1.20-23. The Ascension in Acts is considered as the one condition which makes possible the gift of the Spirit and the miraculous effectiveness of the Apostles' work and witness (see esp. 2.32-33).

We see from v. 6 that the Apostles were still expecting an early accession of political power for Israel. Vv. 7-8 give the corrective to this expectation. They are told that it is not for them to know times or seasons. Their function is to receive power after which they are to be witnesses to Christ in ever-expanding concentric circles, beginning from Jerusalem, and reaching to 'the uttermost part of the earth'.

After the Ascension, and the vision of angels which is recorded as accompanying it (vv. 1-11), the Apostles (eleven of them—Judas being now dead) return to Jerusalem, where they live together, waiting for the gift of the Spirit, alongside of THE WOMEN (i.e. those referred to in Luke 24.10), our Lord's mother, and His brethren who had not been entirely one with Jesus in His earthly life (Mark 3.31ff.; John 7.5), though one of them, James, had received a vision of the risen Lord (I Cor. 15.7). This group, consisting of the Apostles, our Lord's mother, the women, and His own brothers, was the nucleus of the primitive church.

3. the things pertaining to the Kingdom of God

The rule or reign of God had been the core of the preaching and teaching of Jesus, and His miracles had been its demonstration. Luke shows that the post-resurrection

teaching had the same theme. The phrase KINGDOM OF GOD
is not much used in the Epistles, but the underlying idea
continues, even in phrases such as 'eternal life'.

4. being assembled together with them
Possibly the Greek means 'eating with them' or 'living
with them'.

the promise of the Father
Cf. Luke 24.49, 'behold, I send the promise of my Father
upon you'. John the Baptist, according to Luke 3.16, had
indicated that Jesus would baptize with the Holy Ghost and
with fire. Christ here treats the coming baptism with Holy
Spirit as 'the promise of the Father'. John 14.15-17, 26,
treats the Father as the ultimate source of the gift of the
Spirit. Probably by THE PROMISE in this verse (Acts 1.4)
Luke is referring to the Old Testament promises of the
divine gift (see below on 2.14-21).

8. Throughout Acts, the Holy Spirit is thought of as the
means whereby Christians receive power to witness Christ
and His Resurrection.

11. this same Jesus . . . shall so come in like manner as ye have seen him go into heaven
The hope of the return in triumph of the exalted Christ
is not particularly stressed in Acts, but this passage, as well
as a few others (e.g. 3.19-21), shows that it shares the general
New Testament view of this matter. This is that the whole
history of the Church is initiated by the first coming of
Jesus, and will be consummated by His return.

12. a sabbath day's journey
The distance that could be lawfully travelled on the Sab-
bath day, viz. six furlongs (see Ex. 16.29).

13. The list of the apostles (identical with that in Luke

6.14-16, with the omission of Judas Iscariot) differs from
the list in Mark and Matthew in giving JUDAS THE SON OF
JAMES (not 'brother' as in A.V.) instead of Thaddaeus.
Some commentators identify them, but a difference in the
tradition is a more probable explanation.

14. With his brethren

The natural explanation of this phrase is that Mary and
Joseph had children after the birth of Jesus, but from the
early days of the Church other explanations were given,
e.g. that 'brethren' here means 'cousins'. A sense of rever-
ence probably explains the origin of such interpretations.

THE COMPLETION OF THE
APOSTOLIC BAND
1.15-26

The vacant place in the number of the twelve apostles
through the defection of Judas Iscariot has to be filled, and
this is the only event recorded between the Ascension and
the giving of the Spirit on the Day of Pentecost. Notice the
following important points in this section: (1) Peter is
shown as taking the lead from the very start. This clearly
corresponded to the facts. Peter comes first in all the lists
of the apostles, and the words of Jesus recorded in Matt.
16.18 show that his leadership was felt to have Christ's
authority behind it. (2) The O.T. quotations applied by
Peter to Judas (v. 20) show that the re-interpretation of the
O.T. by finding everywhere references to Jesus and to events
connected with His life was from the beginning the main
plank in the platform of the primitive Church. (3) The fact
that a substitute had to be found for Judas shows that 'the
twelve' were thought of as a self-contained group, on a
different footing from other Christians (cf. I Cor. 15.5, 'he
was seen of Cephas, then of the twelve'). (4) One of the

twelve—an apostle in this special sense—had to be one who had 'companied' with Jesus and His disciples during His earthly life, and one who could give personal witness to the Resurrection (vv. 21-22). In this sense the unique apostolic witness could not be repeated—it was a once-for-all testimony—though the *substance* of this witness, and certain apostolic functions in the Christian society, could be handed on to others.

18-19. The account of the fate of Judas has points of agreement and points of disagreement with the account in Matt. 27.3-10. Agreements: Judas came to a violent end. His fate was *somehow* connected with a field known as THE FIELD OF BLOOD. Disagreements: Acts says that he fell headlong (presumably from a rocky ledge); Matthew that he hanged himself. Acts says that he bought the field; Matthew that the chief priests bought it with the money that he returned when stricken with remorse.

20. Free quotations from Pss. 69.25 and 109.8.

22. This verse contains a summary of what is contained in each of the four gospels (though St. Matthew and St. Luke preface their story with the Infancy narratives), and it shows how the Gospels must have been written as permanent records of 'the apostolic witness'.

23. Nothing further is heard in the Bible about Matthias, who was elected to fill Judas's place, or of Barsabas, who was not.

26. Decision by 'lots' was common in Bible times (cf. Mark 15.24, though this instance concerned Gentiles—Romans—not Jews). It is not referred to in the subsequent history of the apostolic church.

THE GIFT OF THE SPIRIT
2.1-13

It would be difficult to exaggerate the importance which Luke attaches to these thirteen verses, and that which he expects his readers to attach to it. They contain an account of that incident without which all the rest of his story would be meaningless. We must try to see why he regards it as so important, and must not allow the difficulties which arise in our modern, critical minds to deflect our interest from the main points. We can surmise that the story is important from at least six points of view.

1. *The Birth of the Spirit-filled Church Corresponds to the Birth of the Spirit-filled Jesus in the Gospel*

This incident stands in the same relation to the rest of the book as the birth of Jesus does to the rest of the Gospel according to St. Luke. The whole story of Christ's birth is told in the context of the Holy Spirit's activity. The Spirit is to fill John the Baptist (Luke 1.15), and to overshadow Mary (Luke 1.35). The Spirit fills Elizabeth (Luke 1.41) and inspires the Song of Zacharias (Luke 1.67). The Spirit assures Simeon of his coming vision of the Lord's Messiah (Luke 2.26). Later, at Christ's baptism (Luke 3.22) the Spirit descends on Jesus 'in bodily shape like a dove'. Christ proceeds to demonstrate the power of the Spirit in His preaching and miracles. Similarly, the birth of the Church is announced to the world with every sign of the presence and power of the Holy Spirit (Acts 2.2-4).

2. *The Baptist's Promise is Fulfilled*

A very important verse in Luke is Luke 3.16: 'one mightier than I cometh . . . he shall baptize you with the Holy Ghost and with fire.' This was itself an echo of many

Old Testament passages promising the gift of God's Spirit, either to the Messiah, or to the whole nation (see, e.g. Isa. 11.2; Ezek. 36.26; Joel 2.28). This promise is emphasized at the end of the gospel (Luke 24.49), and the incident in Acts 2.1-13 is undoubtedly taken as the fulfilment of 'the promise of the Father'.

3. The Pentecostal Gift Corresponds to the Giving of the Law on Mount Sinai

This point does not lie on the surface of the story, but was probably in the mind of Luke. It must always be remembered that the writings of the New Testament are those which record the giving of the new covenant (see Jer. 31.31), and that comparison with the old covenant was very natural (cf. II Cor. 3.5ff.; Heb. 8.13). The Sermon on the Mount in Matt. 5–7 is often thought to represent the giving of a new Law. Now there was a Jewish tradition that at the giving of the Law on Sinai God's voice was heard in every language and it was also held that the Law was given at the Feast of Pentecost (see references in Bruce, *The Acts of the Apostles*, p. 83). The hearing of the gospel in many tongues may have been thought of as the counterpart to the Sinai incident.

4. The Spirit is the Spirit of Testimony to Jesus Christ

In the gospel, it is the Spirit which enables Zacharias and others to proclaim the meaning of the events which they witness. In Acts it is the Spirit which empowers the infant Church to proclaim the apostolic message. The apostles proclaim 'the wonderful works of God', i.e. the events of Calvary and Easter interpreted in the light of prophecy. The rest of Acts is but the continuation of this witness.

5. The Gospel is Proclaimed to the Whole Jewish World

A cross-section of the whole of Jewry is gathered at

Jerusalem for the festival. The Jews were at this time
extensively scattered over the Mediterranean world, and
beyond the Mediterranean to the East, and the 'Dispersion', as it was called, represented the larger and more
influential part of Judaism. Their representatives, as well
as those of Palestine Jewry, are all assembled and form the
audience which hears the first full proclamation of the
apostolic message. The list of countries represented in
vv. 9-11 is worthy of study. It begins with the representatives of Eastern Jewry (Parthians, Medes, Elamites, Mesopotamia), moves west to Judaea, north-west to Cappadocia
and the other districts of Asia Minor, south-west to Egypt
and Libya, west to Rome, and to this long list of countries
Crete and Arabia are added as a kind of postscript. The
list is certainly meant to be an inclusive one. Some have
seen a significance in the number of districts. This is a
precarious calculation, but it is a fact that in the Greek the
list breaks up into seven divisions, and it is also a fact that
the Jews believed that there were seventy languages in
the world. There may be a connection between the two
facts.

6. *St. Luke Records a Miracle of Communication*

Now we come to the point on which attention is usually
focused, the 'speaking with tongues'. Let us see first of all
exactly what Luke relates. He says that CLOVEN TONGUES
LIKE AS OF FIRE set upon each of the apostles, that they BE-
GAN TO SPEAK WITH OTHER TONGUES—apparently meaning in
strange languages—that all those present, no matter where
they came from, understood, in spite of the known fact that
the speakers were all Galileans. Some took the event to
indicate drunkenness. There are certain well-known problems about this story. The chief difficulties are (1) Greek
and Aramaic should have sufficed as means of communica-
tion for all those said to be present. Aramaic itself would
probably have been sufficient. (2) The excitement evinced

and created reminds us of the phenomenon known as *glossolalia,* ecstatic speech often connected with religious excitement, and fairly fully described in I Cor. 14.1-28. (3) The concentration of the story on the fact that the speakers were Galileans suggests that the surprise was that this country dialect (cf. 'broad Scots' in the ears of a Londoner) was not impeding understanding.

It is impossible to get back with certainty to what actually happened. The real choices seem to be (*a*) an outbreak of ecstatic speech, which has been idealized by Luke or his sources, so as to become a miraculous, and presumably temporary command of strange languages; (*b*) such speech on the part of rude Galileans that Jews from all parts could understand, also idealized by Luke to emphasize that the world-wide task of the Church had been undertaken in earnest through the power of the witnessing Spirit.

1. Pentecost

An important festival, representing the completion of the harvest, seven weeks from the Passover.

2, 3. For wind and fire as emblems of the Spirit's power, see Luke 3.17.

10. Jews and proselytes

This apparently refers only to the STRANGERS FROM ROME mentioned immediately before, but it can be taken to apply to all the groups mentioned. The point is that the audience contained Jews by race, and those who had become 'Jews' by religious conversion, accepting the sign of circumcision (if males) and of ceremonial washing (incumbent on males and females). There was an outer circle known as 'God-fearers' who were attracted to Judaism but who had not become legal Jews (see Acts 13.16).

PETER'S SERMON
2.14-36

There now follows Peter's first solemn proclamation of
the Christian gospel. It had been stated by Jesus that Peter
was to be the rock on which the Church was to be built, and
whatever else this promise may have included, it certainly
proved true that he was the leader of the first band of
apostles, and that historically he laid the foundation on
which the subsequent history of the apostolic church was
built. His opening sermon deserves very careful study, for
it contains, in summary form, the essence of the Christian
message.

It divides itself easily into five sections, each of which
contains an important point.

1. *The Strange Phenomena Explained, 14-21*

Peter begins by explaining the strange things that have
been witnessed. THESE MEN ARE NOT DRUNKEN AS YE SUP-
POSE. Far from it. Rather are they the recipients of a
divine gift, none other than that promised centuries before
by the Prophet Joel (see Joel 2.28-32), the gift of God's
own Spirit, promised as an accompaniment of the last days.
St. Peter means that the long expected LAST DAYS have
dawned, and the supernatural prophetic powers of the
apostles are the sign of its arrival.

2. *Responsibility for the Crucifixion Laid on the Jews, 22-23*

The speaker reminds his hearers of Jesus of Nazareth,
and of His miracles, which he takes as a certain sign of
God's favour. But the people of Jerusalem had crucified
and slain Him. The fact that all had happened BY THE
DETERMINATE COUNSEL AND FOREKNOWLEDGE OF GOD in no
way relieved His murderers of guilt. In this passage the
Cross is not clearly interpreted as a sacrifice for sin (although

the ideas of Isa. 53 are never far from the writer's mind).
The stress is rather on the guilty actions of those who
actually engineered Christ's death.

3. *God Reversed Man's Verdict, 24-28*

Peter, as a true apostle, becomes a witness to the Resurrection. God had raised Jesus, reversing the verdict of the
Jews, and fulfilling a striking passage in Ps. 16.8-11. Originally this passage about deliverance from death (THOU WILT
NOT LEAVE MY SOUL IN HELL, i.e. *sheol*, Hades, the place of
the departed) may have referred to escape from death by
recovery from serious illness, but its language was such that
to those who had witnessed the resurrection it spoke at once
of that great deliverance.

4. *Christ, not David, the Subject of Psalm 16, 29-35*

Two points are brought forward as proof that the words
of Ps. 16 can only be properly interpreted of Jesus.
(*a*) David died and was buried: his flesh *did* see corruption
(v. 31). (*b*) David did not ascend, but Jesus did, and the
gift of the Spirit is a sign that He is at God's right hand
(v. 34). The Hebrew of Ps. 16.9 reads 'My flesh also shall
dwell *safely*', i.e. 'it will not be in fear of death'. The
Septuagint rendered this 'shall rest in hope', and it is this
version which Peter is reported as using. This is a rather
clear example of an Old Testament passage, which in its
original setting had no obvious Messianic reference, being
re-interpreted in the light of subsequent events so as to
speak of Christ and His resurrection. The fact that Peter
is recorded as using the Greek version certainly suggests
that the *details* of this speech emanate from a Greek-
speaking *milieu*, but the original psalm certainly expressed confidence in God, in spite of all temptation
to the contrary, and as such was a suitable one with
which to illustrate God's reversal of man's verdict on
Jesus.

5. *The Conclusion: Jesus is Lord and Christ, 36*

This is the substance of the whole apostolic message. Jesus is proved to be Messiah, anointed Saviour and deliverer, and Lord, supreme ruler over all things made by God, exercising the *lordship* which was one of the attributes of the *Lord* God. Peter says GOD HATH MADE THAT SAME JESUS . . . BOTH LORD AND CHRIST, and the words suggest that Jesus had become those things during or after His earthly life. This was not the view of the primitive Church as a whole (see Phil. 2.5-11), although there may have been a period at the beginning of the apostolic history, when the pre-existence of Jesus as Son of God was not clearly grasped.

A few detailed points may be noted.

15. The third hour, i.e. about 9 a.m., too early for feasting.

18. The return of the apparently vanished gift of prophecy was one of the expected signs of the last days.

19-20. There had been no literal fulfilment of these catastrophic signs, but the whole dramatic story of Good Friday to Pentecost corresponded to such upheavals.

23. The foreknowledge of God in connection with the Cross is seen in passages like Isa. 53, which, although not intended as history in advance, foreshadow in various ways the great events of the gospel-history.

25. St. Peter naturally accepts the usual view of his time that David wrote the Psalms.

30. For the divine **oath**, see Ps. 132.11-12.

34. Quotes Ps. 110.1, one of the Old Testament passages most freely quoted in the New.

36. Lord (Greek *kurios*, Aramaic *maran* as in *Maranatha*, I Cor. 16.22, Our Lord Come) was primarily a title for God in the O.T.   *God* stood for God's absolute Being: *Lord* for what He meant for Israel and mankind.

Christ (Messiah, 'anointed') is used in the O.T. of the king, whence it came to be used of that successor to David for whom the Jews looked forward with passionate longing.

A NOTE ON THE APOSTOLIC PREACHING

The sermons or addresses in the early chapters of Acts are important, for they preserve for us the outline of the gospel message as proclaimed by the primitive Church. Examples specially worthy of study are Peter's speech after Pentecost (Acts 2.14-40), Peter's speech after the miracle (Acts 3.12-26), Peter's speech to Cornelius (Acts 10.34-43). The outline of these speeches should be compared with St. Paul's outline of the gospel (I Cor. 15.1-9) and with the outline of the four gospels.   Each of these is, in its own way, an expansion of the gospel message.   That is why St. Mark's Gospel begins, ' The beginning of the gospel of Jesus Christ ', and why St. John's Gospel ends (John 20.31) ' These are written that ye might believe that Jesus is the Christ, the Son of God, and that believing, ye might have life through his name '.

Professor C. H. Dodd, in his book *The Apostolic Preaching and its Developments,* shows that the outline of the message can be traced throughout the New Testament.   The message can be summarized under six points:

1. The last days have dawned.
2. The death and resurrection of Jesus, shown to be in

accord with Old Testament prophecy, have inaugurated 'the last days'.

3. Jesus is now exalted at God's right hand.
4. The Holy Spirit in the Church is the sign of Christ's present power.
5. Christ will shortly return in glory.
6. All those who hear are called on to repent and believe.

It will be noticed that this outline is very similar to that followed in the Apostles' Creed, and as that creed was originally a baptismal confession, the fact is of significance.

It might be thought that all this lay on the surface of the New Testament, but it was not until Dr. Dodd published his book that it was clearly understood. It was he, too, who familiarized in English the Greek word *kerygma* (= proclamation), which is now widely used to describe the content of the primitive Christian gospel.

A later book by Professor Dodd (*According to the Scripture*, Nisbet, 1952) has thrown still more light on the question as to *how* the primitive *kerygma* was built up. He carefully traces those Old Testament passages which are quoted by more than one New Testament author, deducing that they formed part of the very earliest tradition which he can discover. He shows that these passages lead us to certain *sections* of the Old Testament (e.g. Joel 2-31; Zech. 9-14; Dan. 7; Isa. 52.13; 53.12). The whole group of passages he classifies as covering: (*a*) Apocalyptic and eschatological passages, (*b*) Passages relating to the New Israel, (*c*) Passages relating to the Servant of the Lord and the Righteous Sufferer. It will be seen that this expands the material summarized as the outline of the primitive gospel. The last days had dawned—the followers of Jesus were the new, or true Israel—the death and resurrection of Jesus followed the pattern of God's dealings with His Righteous Servant. The book marks a notable step forward in our understanding of the *sources* of the apostolic gospel.

Perhaps we should say ' of the *formulation* of the apostolic gospel ', for the source of the gospel itself was God's action in Jesus Christ. But this action had to be interpreted.

Dr Dodd, in another work (*The Interpretation of the Fourth Gospel*, C.U.P., 1953) provides in a paragraph an excellent summary of the *kerygma*, and it will be seen that his position on this matter has not undergone any essential change.

' The *kerygma* is essentially a proclamation of the facts about Jesus in an eschatological setting which indicates the significance of the facts. It is prefaced, or accompanied, by the announcement that the prophecies are fulfilled in these facts, which must consequently be regarded as inaugurating a new age, and a new order of relations between God and man; and it is attested by an appeal to the experience of the Spirit in the Church. The literary form which came to be known as *euaggelion* is based upon the *kerygma*, and the Fourth Gospel no less than the others. The main topics recur, and in the same order, as they are found in Mark and in the primitive forms of *kerygma* in Acts: the preaching of John the Baptist, the inauguration of Jesus as Messiah, His ministry in Galilee, His removal from Galilee to Jerusalem, His sufferings, death and resurrection, and the coming of the Holy Spirit.'

THE IMMEDIATE CHALLENGE
2.37-40

The crowd are convicted by the force of Peter's words, and confront him with the question, WHAT SHALL WE DO? His answer is clear. (i) Repent, change your attitude fundamentally and (ii) be baptized. Just as John the Baptist had provided a physical washing as a ' prophetic sign ' of the change of heart for which he pleaded, so Peter calls on his hearers to BE BAPTIZED. According to St. Matthew (28.19),

Jesus had told His disciples to baptize their converts, i.e. immerse them in water. Here baptism is IN THE NAME OF JESUS CHRIST, i.e. it means that the converts enter into His obedience, base all their hopes upon Him. Jesus had Himself been baptized, and the baptism had foreshadowed and led to the Cross (cf. Mark 10.38f.; Luke 12.50). Now Christians, by baptism, became united with Christ and entered into the fruits of His death and resurrection. Such baptism is FOR THE REMISSION OF SINS (v. 38) and prepares the way for the gift of the Holy Spirit.

39 foreshadows the wider mission of the Church: THE PROMISE IS UNTO YOU, AND TO YOUR CHILDREN, AND TO ALL THAT ARE AFAR OFF, EVEN AS MANY AS THE LORD OUR GOD SHALL CALL (cf. 1.8).

40. Untoward generation, lit. crooked, out of the right path.

LIFE IN THE PRIMITIVE CHURCH
2.41-47

This passage provides us with the most picturesque account of the life and temper of the primitive Christian community. Notice the main points which are stressed. (i) There was a great influx of converts (three thousand) and these all passed into the Church through the gate of baptism (see above on 2.37-40). (ii) The Church had its organized life under the guidance of the apostles. V. 42 is particularly important. The first uniting bond in the Church was the teaching of the apostles. Doubtless the material which now forms our Gospels was part of the teaching. Evidence from the Old Testament in support of Christian claims was probably prominent. Material such as we find in the Epistles, in so far as it was relevant to a wholly Jewish church, may also have been included. Then there was the *koinōnia*, the

common life. The principal element in this common life
was a mutual responsibility in material things, such as is
described in v. 44, but the common sharing in spiritual
things, notably in the gift of the Spirit, may also be implied.
Further, there was THE BREAKING OF BREAD. The interpretation of this phrase is difficult, because all meals in
Jewish homes began with a solemn breaking of bread
accompanied by thanksgiving—it may be compared to a
rather ceremonial form of saying grace. Sometimes the
phrase is used of a meal which was certainly not, in any
clear sense, the Eucharist (see especially Acts 27.35). At
other times it is used unmistakably of the Eucharist (see
I Cor. 10.16 and Acts 20.7). It is used here (in 2.42) in
close connection with three definitely *religious* matters—
Christian teaching, Christian fellowship and Christian
prayer, which suggests that the phrase stood for something
of a religious character, rather than being a mere synonymn
for taking necessary food. But the distinction between
ordinary food and the Eucharist was not so sharp in primitive times as later. At Corinth abuses occurred just because
the Eucharistic meals were opportunities for ordinary eating; in fact St. Paul's strictures on the Corinthians in this
connection were the first stage in the separation of the
Eucharist from such ordinary meals. So perhaps here a
good paraphrase might be: 'they continued to take food
together, including in their meals the commemoration
which Jesus had enjoined.' Finally they continued in
PRAYERS—first of all the ordinary Temple and Synagogue
prayers, but also doubtless joining in special times of
prayer among themselves. (iii) Powerful actions, similar
to the miracles of Jesus, occurred (v. 43). (iv) A measure
of common ownership of property was adopted (44-45)—not
complete community of goods, for Barnabas and Ananias
and Sapphira still had property to dispose of in chapters 4
and 5. (v) The regular participation in prayer and bread-
breaking is stressed once more, this time with a mention of

the joy which characterized their lives, a joy which proved attractive to ALL THE PEOPLE. (vi) Growth of the Church was a daily phenomenon (v. 47) and was felt to be the result of God's activity—THE LORD ADDED TO THE CHURCH DAILY SUCH AS SHOULD BE SAVED, literally, those who were being saved (to the Church is probably not in the original text, but was put in to explain a different Greek phrase meaning 'together'—R.V. marg. The Lord added together).

II

PROGRESS, DIFFICULTIES AND TRIUMPHS IN JERUSALEM
3–5

A LAME MAN HEALED
3.1-11

Peter and John, associated with James at the Transfiguration and at other great crises in our Lord's Ministry, and found together as a pair in St. John 20.2, and in close relationship to each other in St. John 21.20, are here making their way up to the Temple for prayer. They still observe the regular Jewish hours of prayer, and visit the Temple for the purpose. Seeing a lame beggar being carried to his daily begging site, and being asked for *an alms* (*alms* is singular, from French *almesse*, from Greek *eleēmosynē*) they tell him to rise and walk, just as Jesus had told the paralysed man to do in Mark 2.11. Their command is IN THE NAME OF JESUS CHRIST OF NAZARETH—they speak on Christ's behalf, wielding the authority committed to them more than once. Great amazement naturally followed.

1. ninth hour
   Three o'clock.

2. the gate . . . called Beautiful
   Probably one of the nine gates leading from the Court of the Gentiles to the next Court, that known as the Court of the Women.

11. the porch that is called Solomon's
Solomon's colonnade, running along the east side of the outer Court.

PETER EXPLAINS THE MIRACLE
AND CALLS FOR REPENTANCE
3.12-26

When Peter saw the crowd gathering, he saw that there was an opportunity not to be missed, and the second half of this chapter is devoted to his address. This follows much the same line as his address in chapter 2, but there are some fresh turns in the argument. His first task is to disclaim all personal credit for the miracle (v. 12). The activity which has been evidenced is that of the God of Israel. But the miracle is not an arbitrary expression of benevolent power. It is directly related to the events which have recently taken place in Jerusalem. God has GLORIFIED (exalted, raised to a position of dominance) His servant (SON in A.V. is a mistake for servant—see below on vv. 13 and 26). The Jesus whom God had raised was the very one whom they had rejected.

13-15. The apostles were the witnesses of both events, the rejection, and the Resurrection. Because the apostles believed in God's action in Christ, had FAITH IN HIS NAME, they could, as it were, release His power, to the infinite benefit of the lame beggar (v. 16).

Peter now goes several steps further. The Jews had acted in ignorance (v. 17), but God had overruled their ignorance to make it the means whereby the O.T. prophecies of a suffering Messiah had been fulfilled (v. 18).

19-26 show the unique privilege which had fallen on that generation. They were the heirs of all the promises (v. 25).

By believing on Jesus they could enter into the heritage
prepared by God for His chosen people. THE TIMES OF
REFRESHING could come to pass.

13. His Son Jesus (His Servant Jesus)

The Greek word translated Son (R.V. Servant) is the
word *pais*, a word of very special importance in the Acts
and the New Testament generally. It is used in the LXX
to translate the Hebrew word *'ebedh*, slave or servant, a
word which is constantly used in Isa. 40-53 of the servant
of the Lord, the *pais theou*. While there are many schools
of interpretation offering different meanings of the phrase in
Isaiah, the important thing for us is that it presents a servant
of God (be it Israel, Isaiah himself, or the coming Messiah)
who served by suffering, and whose suffering brought release
and forgiveness to ' the many ' (see especially Isa. 53). Now
these passages from Isaiah were evidently of great value
and importance for the primitive Church. They (1) enabled
them to accept the idea that a crucified Messiah was not a
contradiction in terms: (2) gave them a clue as to *why*
Jesus had had to suffer, viz., to make forgiveness possible.
So when St. Peter calls Jesus *pais*, or servant, he is claiming
all the great prophecies of Isaiah as sources of light on the
mission of Jesus. Hence he stresses, in this sermon, the
innocence of Jesus, the sin involved in His execution, the
possibility of forgiveness (v. 26). The fact that the word
pais is used in this primitive preaching (and its use is a sign
of the antiquity of this material) shows how early the Church
came to understand that Christ's death had been a sacrifice
for sin. Many think that in the words of Jesus recorded in
Mark 10.45 we see evidence that Jesus Himself consciously
assumed the role of the Suffering Servant, and that His
words at the Last Supper give further testimony to the fact
that He regarded His death as a divinely ordained means
of redemption and remission.

(Useful books on the Suffering Servant in Isaiah are:

H. Wheeler Robinson, *The Cross in the Old Testament*,
S.C.M. Press, and H. H. Rowley, *The Servant of the Lord
and other Essays*, Lutterworth Press, also C. R. North, *The
Suffering Servant in Deutero-Isaiah*, O.U.P.)

14. the Holy One and the Just
Two titles for Jesus, both of which had been used in
earlier literature of the Messiah.

a murderer
Of course, Barabbas.

15. the Prince of life
The word translated prince is *archēgos*, which means
leader or pioneer. It occurs in 5.31, also in Heb. 2.10 and
12.2.

16. The grammar of this verse is awkward in both English
and Greek, and many efforts have been made to straighten
it out, but the meaning is clear enough. An Aramaic
original may have been wrongly translated.

18. all his prophets
The principal passages are to be found in the Servant
Songs, but support for the idea of a Suffering Messiah could
be found in various Psalms, as well as in the example of
men like Joseph and Elijah.

19. times of refreshing
(Cf. v. 21, THE TIMES OF RESTITUTION OF ALL THINGS.)
Both phrases are descriptions of ' the good time coming ' to
which the Jews looked forward. Peter associates this with
the return of Jesus, vv. 20, 21.

22. Quotation from Deut. 18.15.

26. Unto you first

Here is another hint that the opportunity now offered to
the Jews will, particularly if rejected by them, pass in time
to others. Acts will show us this happening in successive
stages.

FIRST ARREST AND RELEASE OF
THE LEADING APOSTLES
4.1-31

This chapter tells the story of the first outbreak of opposition to the new message. It came from the official circles
in charge of the Temple, where the miracle had been done
and where the crowd had gathered (3.11). Their anxiety
arose from the fact that they preached THROUGH JESUS THE
RESURRECTION FROM THE DEAD. Doubtless the chief objec-
tion lay in the fact that they preached that Jesus Himself,
whose death the Temple authorities had engineered, had
risen from the dead, but according to the author of Acts
this included from the start the promise that others could
and would share His resurrection. They kept them in ward
for the night (the events of chapter 3 must therefore have
occupied some three hours, as it was 3 p.m. when the
apostles went up to the Temple). Before we are told the
sequel we are assured, in v. 4, that this first check did not
interrupt the victorious movement. 'Nothing can stop the
gospel'—the number of converts rose rapidly to 5,000.

Vv. 5-22 tell the story of the first trial-scene in which
Christians were the defendants, their offence being preaching the gospel. Far from being the last of such trials, they
have continued in various parts of the world until the present
time. Mark 13.9 has thus found ample fulfilment. The
apostles were arraigned before an influential council, pre-
sided over by the High Priest, and as v. 15 calls it THE

COUNCIL (Gk. *sunedrion*=Heb. *sanhedrin*), we must assume
that it was an official meeting of the Sanhedrin, the council
of seventy members, which in N.T. times wielded considerable power in Jerusalem. Faced by a direct challenge (v. 7)
Peter is FILLED WITH THE HOLY GHOST (v. 8) as he makes his
reply, thus giving proof of the fulfilment of Christ's promise
recorded in Mark 13.11. The Holy Spirit is pre-eminently
the Spirit of witness, enabling men to testify to the work of
Christ. The substance of Peter's speech is similar to that of
the speech made the day before in the Temple. The miracle
had been done, he says, in the name of Jesus Christ of
Nazareth, and he does not forget to add that this Jesus is
He whom they crucified. God had raised Him, thus fulfilling in the most striking way the 'prophecy' of Ps. 118.22,
in which a rejected stone becomes after all THE HEAD OF THE
CORNER. V. 12 makes the bold assertion that only in His
name—through trust and obedience to Him—is salvation
to be found. The Council was amazed at the eloquence
and boldness of the two Galilean fishermen, but on closer
attention to them recalled that they had been companions
of Jesus. Only the presence of the healed man (v. 14) compelled them to take a cautious line, and they decided to let
the apostles off with a caution (17-18). Peter and John
rejected all their demands for silence, and returned to their
own company.

The story of their return (23-31) is vividly told. When
they recount what has happened to them, the hearers (presumably a group of which the remaining apostles were the
nucleus) break out into a spontaneous prayer, the terms of
which give us a good idea of what prayers were like in the
primitive Church (24-30). Notice (*a*) the address—to God
the Creator (v. 24). (*b*) The belief that the O.T. was a means
by which the Holy Spirit had foreshadowed the events which
had recently taken place (25-26, a passage which follows on
aptly after Luke's account of the co-operation of Pilate and
Herod in the Passion story). (*c*) The repeated description

of Jesus as Servant (*pais*, vv. 27, 30). (*d*) The prayer for
boldness, and for the credentials which further mighty works
could provide (29-30). After the prayer, there followed
another striking manifestation of the presence of God's
Spirit, a 'little Pentecost', so similar to the first, that some
have thought we have here another version of the Pentecost
story, wrongly taken by Luke as a new event.

1. captain of the Temple
A very high-ranking official, in charge of the Temple and
the Temple courts.

Sadducees
The party to which the priestly families belonged, mostly
known for their conservatism in religious beliefs (they rejected later Jewish beliefs, e.g. immortality) and their hard-
headed realism in retaining what political power they
could.

6. Annas
Actually ex-High Priest at this time, though his prestige
was so high that in Luke 3.2 he is coupled with Caiaphas,
as though they were both High Priests. Caiaphas was
High Priest at this time.

11. Ps. 118.22 (see above).

12. Salvation (Greek *sōtēria*)
The root meaning of this word is first *deliverance*, as
through victory in battle : I Sam. 9.16: 'a man . . . shall
save my people out of the hands of the Philistines '; then
particularly the deliverance brought or promised by God
to His oppressed people, e.g. Isa. 43.3; 45.21, 22, or to all
the world, Isa. 49.6. In the N.T. it is used of the expected
Messianic deliverance (Luke 2.30) and of the spiritual blessing of forgiveness (Luke 19.9). In the passage under dis-

cussion (Acts 4.12) it is used in an inclusive sense, including physical and spiritual, personal and corporate, present and future deliverance and well-being.

20. We cannot but speak the things which we have seen and heard
The essential task of the apostles is just this task of bearing honest and faithful witness.

25. Ps. 2.1-2.

27. Gentiles
A reference to the Roman share in the Crucifixion.

28.
In the early chapters of Acts it is held that the death of Christ was comprised within the purpose of God, though it is not made clear that the purpose which it was to achieve would be the forgiveness of man's sin. (Cf. Acts 2.23, and for a hint of the fuller doctrine, Acts 13.38-9.)

30. holy child Jesus
Cf. note on 3.13.

GENEROSITY—TRUE AND FALSE
4.32–5.11

We now have another summary of the state of affairs in the primitive Church of Jerusalem not unlike that at the end of chapter 2. Here, however, special stress is laid on the *unity* of the Church, and on the practical expression of that unity in the sharing of worldly goods (v. 32). The claim of the community on personal possessions was considered absolute—NEITHER SAID ANY OF THEM THAT OUGHT OF THE THINGS WHICH HE POSSESSED WAS HIS OWN—but this did not imply an immediate pooling of all property. It does

seem to have implied that the substantial property-owners
sold their lands or houses and gave in the proceeds (v. 34);
though the fact that Barnabas's gift is singled out for mention may mean that such cases were not quite as common
as the verse implies. This view makes it easier to understand how Ananias and Sapphira still had the land
which they sold, and of which they retained part of
the price, while pretending to be handing over the whole
(5.1-8).

The two stories, that of Barnabas and that of Ananias and
Sapphira, must be read together. They show the working
of the Holy Spirit in inspiring self-sacrifice and the
spirit of mutual dependence, and also the activity of the
spirit of evil, which could infect members of the Church,
and turn even a good impulse into an opportunity for self-
glorification and deception. A separate note is added
on the special difficulties of the story of Ananias and
Sapphira.

35. The apostles are clearly regarded as the central administrative authorities of the Church.

36. Scholars have not succeeded in discovering how the
Aramaic **Barnabas** can be interpreted as 'son of consola-
tion' (='the encourager'), but perhaps this was a later
name given to him in addition to the name Barnabas.

Levite
Member of a family with the hereditary right to certain
Temple offices.
Barnabas was of course a Jew, but his family came from
Cyprus.

3. Lying to the apostles is considered lying to the Holy
Spirit, so sure were the early Christians of the presence of
the Spirit in their midst.

Difficulties in the story of Ananias and Sapphira
There are two. Did it happen? If it did, ought it to
have happened? We could call these two problems the
historical and the moral.

(a) *The historical problem*
As incidents like that here described do not happen in
our daily experience we do not find the story easy to believe.
Even if there are some stories in Acts which had grown up
without sound historical foundation, that would not under-
mine our faith in the book as a whole. This story might be
one of this type. On the other hand, in days gone by, many
things happened which would not be expected to-day in
civilized lands. Simple people (such as still exist, e.g. in
parts of Africa) are even to-day much more susceptible to
psychic influence than are their sophisticated contempor-
aries. Cases have been known quite recently where the
threat of death has been sufficient to induce death. If this
can happen to-day, the story takes on a new light, and is
seen to be by no means impossible.

(b) *The moral problem*
Assuming the literal truth of the story (and it is difficult
to see any other possible truth, apart from literal truth),
were these two well-meaning but weak people hardly
treated? Certainly most of us would have had short lives
if every half-truth or deception had been as severely dealt
with! But the early days of the Church were extremely
critical, and it may be that St. Peter was right to take a
severe view of deception at the very heart of the common
life of the Church. It is not for us to judge Peter (or
Ananias and Sapphira) in a superior way, but only to see
how the corruption of the best leads to the worst, and to
learn the importance of absolute honesty and sincerity in
all our expressions of religious devotion. In any case the
main point of the story is to show the supernatural power

which was working in the Church. 4.33 told of GREAT POWER
and GREAT GRACE; 5.11 tells of GREAT FEAR. All these mani-
festations are described by Luke to show that something
really exceptional was at work in the life of the primitive
Church.

A WAVE OF HEALING MIRACLES
5.12-16

Just as in the life of Jesus His fame as a wonder-working
healer spread around, leading to requests for healing on
the part of great crowds (see, e.g., Luke 5.15), so now very
many were anxious to secure the benefit of healing at the
hands of the apostles. In some this took the rather superstitious form of putting their sick friends where Peter's
shadow might fall on them as he passed. Whatever else
this shows, it shows how pre-eminent was Peter's position
as the leader of the apostolic band.

ANOTHER ARREST, ESCAPE, TRIAL
AND DELIVERANCE
5.17-42

The story now told bears marked similarity to that in
chapter 4, except that this time the apostles, after arrest,
escape miraculously, resume preaching, and are re-arrested
and brought before the Sanhedrin. Another difference is
that on the first occasion they are let go without punishment, whereas this time they are beaten before they are
released. Though the section is a long one, there is not
much that need be said apart from those points (of which
there are a good many) which call for detailed notes. The
story is clearly intended to illustrate the theme of the whole
book, ' Nothing can stop the Gospel '.

17. Sadducees

The party which dominated the Temple administration—
old-fashioned in belief, worldly and temporizing in policy.

19. the angel of the Lord by night opened the prison doors

St. Luke never hesitates to attribute historical events to
the intervention of angels (see, e.g., Luke 1.11; 1.26; 2.9;
22.43; Acts 12.7). Evidently he, and the circles from whom
he drew his information, shared the view that God's ' messengers ' were used to mould the shape of events in this way.
We should be wise (1) to realize that similar events may be
described very differently by people of different centuries or
different continents, and that the different explanations do
not mean that there is nothing needing to be explained at
all; (2) to remember that there are ' more things in heaven
and earth ' than we have yet fully realized. We may rightly
regard the conventional angel of medieval art as a mytho-
logical conception, but we need not rush to the other extreme
and assume that the only living beings in God's universe are
man and ' the beasts that perish '.

26. The meaning apparently is ' They brought them in a
quiet courteous manner, lest their popularity should result
in them (i.e. the Temple police) being attacked by the
crowd '. (There are other possible interpretations of the
Greek.)

28. Ye . . . intend to bring this man's blood upon us

The Jewish leaders had grasped one of the main points
of the apostles' message, viz., that the crucifixion had been
a terrible crime for which official Judaism was responsible.

29-32. This is an excellent summary of the apostolic
proclamation, or *kerygma* as it is called in Greek. Notice
the points (*a*) Jesus was sent by God, **the God of our fathers**,
i.e. Abraham, Isaac and Jacob. (*b*) The Jews had killed the

one sent by God. (c) God had exalted Him to be **Prince**
(see note on 3.15) and Deliverer. (d) The call now was to
repent and receive forgiveness. (e) The witness was one in
which the apostles were co-operating with the Holy Spirit,
which had been given to those who accepted the message.

34. Gamaliel

A leading Rabbi (exponent of the Law) under whom St.
Paul studied as a young man (see Acts 22.3). Other things
known about him show that his instincts were on the side
of liberal tolerant views, as appear in this famous speech.
The Pharisees were in conflict with the Sadducees about
many things, and the fact that the Sadducees were so hostile
may have encouraged Gamaliel to take a different line.

35-39. The main point of Gamaliel's speech is clear enough.
He says, 'Don't act in a hurry. Time will prove whether
God is behind this or not.' Not a very courageous line, but
one which we are all prone to follow from time to time.

36-37. These two verses contain some awkward historical
points.
  (a) Theudas, according to Josephus (*Antiquities*, 20.5.1),
      led his revolt at some time after A.D. 44, and therefore
      could not have been mentioned by Gamaliel in this
      way at this early date—about A.D. 31 or 32.
  (b) Judas of Galilee rebelled in A.D. 6, in connection with
      the Census. He therefore should have been mentioned
      before Theudas. While various roundabout solutions
      have been thought of, the easiest view is that Luke
      (or his authority) had no exact report of Gamaliel's
      speech, and that in the editorial process of writing it,
      errors crept in, perhaps originating in a careless use of
      Josephus's *Antiquities*. The strong argument for this
      is that Josephus, lower on the same 'page' as that on
      which he mentions Theudas, refers to the *grandsons* of

Judas. Did Luke overlook the word 'grandsons'? (This last point can be valid only if Acts is very late, after A.D. 93.)

41. Joy in persecution is commanded in the gospels (St. Matt. 5.11-12) and in the Epistles (I Pet. 4.13 and 16) and is evidenced in Acts, both here and in Acts 16.25.

42. they ceased not to teach and preach Jesus Christ
    Broadly speaking, teaching (*didache*) was addressed to Christians; preaching (*kerygma,* or the publication of the evangel) was addressed to those whom the apostles wished to convert.

III

PROGRESS, DIFFICULTY AND TRIUMPH IN THE GREEK-SPEAKING SYNAGOGUES
6 and 7

THE GREEK-SPEAKING CHRISTIAN JEWS ASSERT THEMSELVES
6.1-8

These eight verses probably record an event of outstanding significance in the life of the primitive Church. This event is the emergence of the Greek-speaking element in the Church as a separate force, with a partially different emphasis in their belief and their teaching. This event was one of the results of the rapid increase in the numbers belonging to the Christian Church (6.1, WHEN THE NUMBER OF THE DISCIPLES WAS MULTIPLIED). The occasion, according to our present record, was a complaint on the part of the 'Hellenists' (Greek-speaking Jewish Christians) that their widows were being neglected in the daily ministration. The Christians had naturally taken over the custom of charitably supporting those of their members who could not support themselves, especially the widows. To the Hellenists, it seemed that 'the Hebrews' (Aramaic-speaking Jewish Christians) had favourable treatment. Such complaints usually indicate a falling apart on other and wider issues. Probably the chief among these was the degree of attachment to the Jerusalem Temple and to all the observances of the Jewish Law. We have seen that the first Christians continued to keep the Temple hours of worship (3.1). There is a good deal to suggest that the Hellenist Christians were more critical of the Temple, and more detached from it (see below). The superficial reader might think that the seven men who were appointed as the result of this dispute were just general administrators or 'quartermasters' appointed to relieve the apostles, but it is significant that all the seven new officers bear Greek names. It is natural to think that these seven men were given some standing in association with the apostles, and it is noteworthy, that although they were appointed to SERVE TABLES, what we actually hear of them doing is preaching the gospel just like apostles or evangelists. They are not called 'deacons', although it is implied that they are appointed to serve (Greek, *diakonein*) tables. This appointment is perhaps intended to foreshadow the later order of deacons (Phil. 1.1).

1. Grecians

The Greek word is *Hellenistes,* and although scholars have argued about its exact meaning, the meaning 'Greek-speaking Jew' seems to give the best sense.

Hebrews

If GRECIANS is taken as above, this word seems here to imply 'Hebrew- (i.e. Aramaic) speaking'.

2. The word of God

i.e., the proclamation of the gospel.

5. The whole multitude did the choosing and the apostles laid hands on those chosen (see v. 6).

Stephen and Philip form the main subjects of the two following chapters (7 and 8). Nothing more is heard about the other five, but notice that Nicolas is described as 'a proselyte of Antioch '—i.e. he was not a Jew by birth, but by conversion.

7. This is the only case where we read of the priests becoming Christians, and some scholars think there is a mistake in the text at this point.

8. This verse focuses our attention on Stephen, named first in the list of ' the seven ', and the subject of the next portion of the book.

RESISTANCE FROM THE GREEK-SPEAKING SYNAGOGUES
6.9-15

This little section is important. Just as there are ' foreign ' churches in London, there were synagogues in Jerusalem for groups of Jews with home connections in different parts of the Roman Empire. The emergence of a strong, organized Greek-speaking group in the Church made it possible for Christian activity to take place among members of these synagogues, and vigorous resistance broke out among them too. Possibly Saul of Tarsus was a member of the Cilician Synagogue. The charges brought against Stephen (that he spoke against MOSES, i.e. against the Law, and that he prophesied the destruction of the Temple) suggest that the Hellenist Christians preached a more drastic form of Christianity than the Hebraist Christians had done. Stephen is brought before the Sanhedrin, and makes a remarkable impression on them. Possibly v. 15 is an anticipation of the moment, described in 7.55-56, when Stephen has a vision of Jesus standing at God's right hand.

9. Libertines
Freed slaves, who seem to have formed a special group, almost like a national or provincial grouping.

Alexandrians

Perhaps among some of these we should have found the first missionaries to the great city of Alexandria, where Apollos (see 18.24) probably heard the gospel, perhaps in a rather inadequate form.

11. suborned

Prompted, 'instigated men to give false evidence'. Notice carefully the exact charges against Stephen. He is said to have spoken blasphemous words AGAINST MOSES, AND AGAINST GOD, and later (v. 14) these charges are expanded to include statements against the Temple and the Law, and a prophecy of the coming destruction of the Temple of the Jews. There are several references in the Gospels to a similar charge against Jesus Himself (see Mark 14.58; John 2.19. The latter passage put the words into the mouth of Jesus Himself.) Possibly the historical origin of the charge is to be found in the words of Jesus in Mark 13.2, possibly in a claim by our Lord to supersede the Temple, and to inaugurate the New Covenant (see Matt. 12.6, Mark 14.24). In any case there is a new emphasis in the charge —the Hellenists, and Stephen in particular, are charged with a definitely hostile attitude to Jewish institutions. In Stephen's speech (which follows in chapter 7) we shall see a measure of justification for the charge. Possibly we see here an anticipation of St. Paul's strong stand for the freedom of Christians from the claims of the Jewish Law. Probably the 'Judaisers'—Paul's principal opponents within Christianity—were in closer continuity with the primitive circle of Galilean Christians, though these may have broadened with the lapse of time, and left the party around James as a specially conservative 'pro-Moses' group within the Church.

STEPHEN'S DARING REPLY TO
THE SANHEDRIN
7.1-53

(*Author's note to younger readers*

Most young people, when set to study this chapter for homework or an essay, suffer from alarm and despondency! This is natural, for it seems such a long speech (three columns of small print in my Bible) and contains such a lot of unfamiliar names. Also it seems rather remote, even from its context in Acts. Why ever did Stephen, when fighting for his life, have to go back to Abraham and Moses? The answers to these questions will become clear in the commentary, but meanwhile I want to suggest the best way of tackling the problem. *First,* read the paragraphs below about the nature and substance of the speech. *Secondly,* read the speech itself—preferably in the clear translation of the New English Bible—not worrying too much about individual verses. Just get the general argument. *Thirdly,* go through it carefully, with the detailed notes given below. You will find that it is not nearly so long or so boring as it looks! R.R.W.)

This speech of Stephen is very important because it shows one line of Christian propaganda and apologetic adopted in the early Church. It has special similarities to the point of view of the Epistle to the Hebrews, as well as to some of the teaching of St. Paul. It is important to see its general drift before studying it in detail.

Its main point is that the leaders of the Jews have no right to claim to be the true followers of Moses. Actually, in his own day, Moses' leadership had not been always welcome—both at the beginning of his work, and at later times, his leadership had been rejected. The Jews of Stephen's day, in rejecting Jesus, had been the followers of those who rejected Moses rather than of Moses himself.

All the rest is secondary, but not unrelated to this main theme. Stress is laid throughout on the fact that God's people had been called to live a nomadic life, and that in various degrees they had been able to receive His blessing while in that state. When, however, they settled down—either in Egypt or in Canaan—they developed wrong ideas of the will of God. One of the chief of these wrong ideas was the false importance which they attached to the out-ward Temple—this was in line with the charge made against Stephen by the Council. The Temple, according to Stephen, should not have been thought of as God's dwelling-place. God was more interested in the hearts of His people, which were in fact rebellious. They had persecuted the prophets, and now they had killed Him of whom the prophets told. The teaching is very similar to that in the parable of the wicked husbandmen. (Mark 12.1-12.)

A brief analysis of the speech may be helpful, but it is a mistake to expect to find in it a precise, logical argument.

1-8. God's call to Abraham.

9-19. How the Israelites came to be in Egypt.

20-29. Unhappy start to Moses' career.

30-36. God's revelation to Moses, and the deliverance brought to Israel through him.

37-43. Israel's disobedience in the wilderness.

44-50. The replacement of the Tabernacle (tent of meeting) by the Temple.

51-53. Direct accusation brought against the accusers.

2. before he dwelt in Charran
i.e. while he was in Ur of the Chaldees. Both places are

in Mesopotamia, more or less equivalent to the modern
Iraq. See Gen. 11.31.

3-6. Stephen stresses that Abraham lived by faith and not
by sight, depending only on God's promises. Cf. Heb.
11.8-10. For God's promises to Abraham see, e.g., Gen. 12.7;
13.15; 15.13, etc.

9. The envy of Joseph entertained by the patriarchs is one
of the first signs in Hebrew history of a decline from God's
will, leading to the rejection of one whom God has chosen.
For the story, see Gen. 37.

16. Sychem
   In Samaria (modern Nablus).

17. the promise
   Is that referred to in v. 5.

23. to visit his brethren
   i.e. to consider their situation. For the story, see Exodus
   2.11-15.

25. This is the next failure on the part of the Hebrews, their
failure to accept and recognize Moses as an arbitrator in the
quarrel.

29. Madian
   Means Midian.

30. For the story of the burning bush, see Exodus 3.2.

33. The fact that the burning bush was HOLY GROUND fits in
with Stephen's aim to show that the Divine Presence was
not confined to the Temple. God could reveal Himself any-
where.

35. This Moses

We are now coming to the core of the discussion. It is THIS MOSES—the rejected arbitrator—who is chosen by God to be the Deliverer. The parallel to the case of Jesus must have begun to be obvious to the Sanhedrin.

36.

After the WONDERS AND SIGNS ('the plagues') Moses delivered Israel by bringing them across the Red Sea. After the healing ministry, Jesus had 'redeemed his people' by His death and resurrection.

37. A prophet shall the Lord your God raise up unto you of your brethren

Deut. 18.15. Stephen implies that as Moses was rejected, so has been the Prophet (i.e. Jesus) of whom he spoke.

38. in the church in the wilderness

In the assembly (*ecclesia* usually means the assembly, or the nation as a whole, in the Greek O.T.). See Deut. 18.16 —the verse following the quotation referred to in note above.

the angel which spake to him

Late Jewish tradition held that the Law was given through angels. See v. 53, and Gal. 3.19.

lively oracles

Notice that Stephen does not disparage the Law itself. Cf. St. Paul, Romans 7.12.

41. they made a calf

See Exod. 32.4-6.

42.

God punishes sin by allowing sinners to fall into more sin. See Romans 1.24, 26, 28.

42-43. Have you offered to me . . . sacrifices

This is a difficult passage, popular with examiners, because there are several points to remember. It comes from Amos 5. 25ff. In the original Hebrew, the point was: Israel did *not* offer sacrifices in the wilderness, which shows that sacrifices were not essential. But they *have* indulged in the worship of *Siccuth* and *Chiun* (or perhaps it means they will have to carry these idols into captivity with them as a punishment). Both *Siccuth* and *Chiun* are names for the planet Saturn. The LXX altered *Sikkuth* to *skēnē*, meaning tabernacle, and brought in Moloch for 'your king' (Heb.: *Malkekem*). They also somehow turned the Hebrew *Chiun* into *Remphan*, probably by accidentally mistaking the Hebrew characters. The detailed literary puzzles are not important for the ordinary reader, except that they show fairly plainly that Acts 7 was written by a man using the Greek O.T. and not the Hebrew.

44. tabernacle of witness

O.T. phrase for tabernacle as containing the tables of the Law. Num. 17.7.

according to the fashion that he had seen

Cf. Heb. 8.5. This is one of many links between the thought of Stephen's speech and Hebrews.

45. Jesus

Read Joshua.

46. God of Jacob

Read *house of Jacob*.

47.

Solomon is not severely condemned, for it is Solomon's own speech which is quoted in v. 49. But there is a clear hint that the attempt to locate the presence of God in one building was wrong.

51-53. In violent language, reminiscent of the prophets, Stephen accuses the council of following in the worst steps of their forefathers. They have slain **the just one**, a phrase for Jesus used also in 3.14 and 22.14. They have had the Law, but have not kept it.

THE DEATH OF THE FIRST MARTYR
7.54-59

The council could not stand such devastating criticism. They burst out into what we should now call 'boos and hisses', but this was the occasion of a remarkable incident. Stephen was 'full of the Holy Ghost', i.e. quite transported by the Spirit of God. He looked up and saw in vision the glory of God and Jesus standing on God's right hand. It was the claim of Jesus at His trial that His accusers would see 'the Son of Man' (see below) coming on the clouds of heaven (Mark 14.62), and this was the point at which He was finally condemned. Now Stephen says that he actually sees something very like what Jesus had foretold. He announces what he sees as a vision of heaven opened. The figure at God's right hand, whom he recognizes as Jesus, is also described as 'Son of Man'. This was a phrase used in Daniel 7.13-14 to describe a heavenly figure (who probably symbolizes Israel in that context) who is brought near to God and given universal dominion. Stephen says that Jesus has been called to fill this sacred and honoured role. They rushed on him, cast him out of the city and stoned him, the Jewish method of execution. The Romans were not consulted as far as we know: if not, the execution (or lynching) was irregular. Pilate should have been approached. Two things stand out in the final scene. (1) Saul is present, and plays some minor role, perhaps guarding the clothes of those engaged on the stoning. He 'consented' to Stephen's death, which may mean that he was a member of the Council, and voted for it (cf. Acts 26.10). (2) Stephen shows the same spirit of love and concern for his persecutors as Jesus had done (see Luke 23.34).

58. The witnesses laid down their clothes, etc.

There is evidence from the Mishna that the victim of a stoning was stripped before the execution, but none about the executioners having to strip. Probably this was just for practical convenience, though some have suggested altering the Greek to make it read 'laid down *his* clothes'. If this were correct, it would explain what a vivid sense of guilt and responsibility Paul felt in connection with Stephen's death.

59. Notice that Stephen prays to Jesus, and calls Him **Lord**, the regular O.T. name for God. He does not necessarily identify Him with God, at whose right hand He stands.

IV

PROGRESS IN SAMARIA AND TOWARDS THE SOUTH
8

SEQUELS TO STEPHEN'S DEATH
8.1-4

This little section is clearly intended by the author to bridge the gap between the death of Stephen and the next 'leap forward', which is to take the gospel to Samaria. The different points are rather closely interlocked, but the three main items stand out clearly enough. They are: (1) the burial of Stephen (v. 2). (2) The persecution which followed the incident, Saul playing a part both in the incident itself and in the subsequent wider persecution (vv. 1 and 3). (3) The wider opportunities of preaching the gospel which came as the result of the persecution (v. 4).

1a. Saul was consenting unto his death
The word for consenting (*suneudokoun*) does not imply an official vote, but merely the fact that Saul agreed with the action. The same word is used in 22.20, while in 26.10 the phrase is 'gave my voice' (gave my vote. R.V.). Even the last phrase does not necessitate, although it may imply, a formal vote, such as a member of the Sanhedrin might give. Paul himself testifies to his persecuting activity in I Cor. 15.9.

1b. There was clearly a new outbreak of persecution after the Stephen incident. This is referred to again in 11.19.

The phrase **except the apostles** is strange. It may conceal a reference to the fact that the chief victims of the new attack were those of Stephen's persuasion, and that the apostles—and, we must presume, their immediate circle—being more conservative, were spared in this particular outbreak. *The regions of Judaea and Samaria* indicate a widening of the range of evangelistic work, of which we are to hear in more detail in vv. 5ff.

4. This verse is fully in line with what we have said is the theme of Acts: 'Nothing can stop the gospel.'

THE MISSION TO SAMARIA
8.5-25

These verses describe Philip's mission to Samaria, the territory to the north of Judaea (the capital city was some forty miles from Jerusalem). The story is particularly important. (1) It represents not only a geographical advance but an advance in the type of audience which was being addressed. Samaritans were looked on as a kind of half-caste by the Jews (see John 4.9). Luke, on the other hand, always presented the Samaritans in a good light (see Luke 10.33, and Luke 17.16). Their evangelization was a step on the way to the evangelization of Gentiles. (2) It shows that Philip, listed immediately after Stephen in the seven, was also more of a preacher than an administrator. (3) It raises an interesting point as to just why Peter and John went down to follow up Philip's work—see notes on 14-17.

5. the city of Samaria
The true text of the Greek may mean 'a city of Samaria', not Samaria, the capital, which by this time was called Sebaste.

preached Christ

Notice this brief summary of what Christian evangelization meant. Cf. Phil. 1.15-16.

7-8. Signs similar to those which accompanied our Lord's work, and that of the apostles, follow the preaching.

9. This verse introduces the story of Simon the Sorcerer. Notice (looking ahead for a moment) what happens. (*a*) Simon deceives the people by his magic, (*b*) Simon accepts the gospel (v. 13), (*c*) Simon is tempted by envy when he sees the apostles' power to convey the gift of the Spirit and seeks to obtain the same gift by bribery, (*d*) condemned by Simon Peter (vv. 20ff.), he repents and begs Peter's prayers. The point of the story lies in the contrast between Simon's conception of spiritual power, which both before and after his conversion amounted to little more than profitable conjuring, and the true exhibition of the power of Christ, who was Lord over all spiritual powers, by Philip and the apostles.

10. This man is the great power of God

Read, with R.V. 'This man is that power of God which is called Great.' Many inscriptions have been found from these times referring to a 'great power' of God or the gods.

12. the things concerning the Kingdom of God

Notice how this phrase is now defined more closely by the addition of the words **and the name of Jesus Christ**. The general message of John the Baptist and our Lord Himself had now crystallized into the specific message concerning Christ and His Power.

14-17. This visit of the apostles to Samaria is of course very important. The account is too brief for us to know exactly why they made the journey. Perhaps they wanted to make sure that the new evangelistic movement was kept closely

linked to the original church of Jerusalem. Perhaps they were
not quite sure yet whether to admit Samaritans on equal
terms with full Jews. Whatever the purpose, the *result* is
clearly described. They laid their hands on the converts
and this led to a receiving of **the holy ghost**, no doubt
similar in its manifestation to the earlier receptions recorded
in chapters 2 and 4. The Church of England looks back to
this incident as one of the main apostolic precedents for
Confirmation. Acts suggests that the gift could only come
through the apostles, but notice that in 19.6, St. Paul—not
one of the Twelve—performs a similar function for the group
of converts at Ephesus.

23. gall of bitterness
i.e. bitter gall, probably referring to a poisonous plant,
e.g. poppy-heads. To be **in** it meant to be in a situation
with bitter possibilities.

25. many villages of the Samaritans
After their successful visit, they continue the good work
on the return journey. Thus, as often, what has been the
goal of missionary effort becomes in its turn a new standing-
point. (Cf. Antioch, Rome, Canterbury, Dornakal.)

A MISSIONARY FOR AFRICA?
8.26-40

It is well known that Acts relates in the main only one
line of missionary advance, that from Jerusalem westwards
to Rome. There must have been many advances in other
directions. Here we have a hint of an advance south-west,
to what we now call the Sudan. The story concerns Philip,
so it naturally comes in here, after Philip's successful
Samaritan mission. Under divine guidance, Philip goes to
the road which led from Jerusalem to Gaza, and thence to

Egypt and Africa. On this road he is used to convert a
courtier of the Ethiopian queen, evidently a proselyte, i.e.
a Gentile convert to the Jewish faith. He has been to
Jerusalem to worship, and is reading Isaiah's prophecy in
his CHARIOT (perhaps an ox-waggon!) on his way home.
After Philip's explanation of what he is reading, he asks for
baptism, receives it, and GOES ON HIS WAY REJOICING. We
are surely meant to imagine him carrying his new faith into
yet another so far unevangelized area.

26. angel of the Lord
Probably Luke means the same here as he does in vv. 29
and 39, when he says THE SPIRIT OF THE LORD, i.e. God,
making His will clearly known in Philip's heart and conscience.

27. Candace
A title for the Ethiopian queen-mother.

32-35. Most important verses. It is Isa. 53.7-8 which the
Eunuch is reading. Philip preaches Jesus to him, beginning
at this passage. This is one of the plainest cases in the N.T.
where the work of Jesus is explained in terms of the Suffering Servant of Isa. 53. Cf. Luke 22.37. It was probably
from this identification that the Church derived its clear
understanding that the death of Jesus was God's way of
bringing release and redemption to mankind. But according to Mark 10.45 our Lord Himself held this view, and
taught it to His disciples.

37. This verse probably was not in the earliest MSS. of
Acts, as it is found only in the so-called *Western* texts (see
note at end of book). But even if not original it is very
early, and gives us an important example of the primitive
baptismal confession. Our creeds began as confessions of
this sort.

38. Even in an unusual situation of this sort, baptism is considered necessary, and as usual in the early Church, it is carried out in the open air, in this case at an oasis or *wadi* or water-track.

39. Luke treats Philip's departure as miraculous.

40. Azotus
Twenty miles north.

Caesarea
Roman headquarters for the Province of Judaea.

V

SAUL THE ARCH-ENEMY IS WON
FOR CHRIST
9.1-31

This passage records one of the most important events in
the whole history of the apostolic age. It is perhaps the
supreme example of the writer's theme that 'nothing can
stop the gospel'. For here we have the outstanding enemy
of the Church suddenly arrested by the direct action of the
Risen Lord and turned into the greatest missionary, and
one of the greatest Christian thinkers of all time. Before
dealing with detailed points, two special topics may be
considered.

(a) Problems of history raised by this passage
We are not concerned here with the historical value and
meaning of the event itself (for that see immediately below),
but with certain apparent inconsistencies between this passage, and passages relating to the same event in other parts
of the New Testament. (i) *Other statements in Acts.* The
conversion of Saul is recorded not only here but in Acts
22.1-21 and Acts 26.1-20. There are differences of detail
between the three accounts, but the only important difference is that in the last of the three passages no mention is
made of Ananias. Instead, Saul appears to receive his
commission of apostleship in the original incident on the
Damascus Road. While this may represent an alternative
and earlier version of the story, in this commentator's view
it can be sufficiently explained by the fact that the author
did not want to go through every detail three times, but

preferred to 'telescope' the later part of the story by going
straight from the sudden experience on the Damascus Road
to the sequel, viz., the commission to take the gospel to the
Gentiles. (ii) *Statements in St. Paul's Epistles*. These raise
more serious problems. In the first place, being statements
by St. Paul himself, they must carry great weight, and
in the event of a direct contradiction between St. Paul and
Acts we must accept St. Paul's account. Secondly the
apparent contradictions are not on matters of detail, but on
points of considerable importance. The Pauline passages
concerned are Gal. 1.11-24 and II Cor. 11.32-33. The
Galatian passages raise the following difficulties. (1) The
claim to have received the message direct from Jesus Christ
can be held to be at variance from the Acts account, which
makes Ananias play an important part. (2) Acts 9, which
says that Saul stayed in Damascus for MANY DAYS, and
then went to Jerusalem cannot easily be reconciled with
Galatians, which describes his immediate journey to Arabia.
(3) The Galatians statement (Gal. 1.22) which says that St.
Paul was 'unknown by face' to the Churches of Judaea
seems to clash with the Acts story (Acts 9.28-29) telling of
his bold preaching in Jerusalem. All that can be said is
that the clash is not quite as severe if it is assumed that Acts
has just ignored the Arabian journey, and if stress is laid
on the fact that Galatians refers to the Churches of *Judaea*,
while Acts refers to the Church of Jerusalem itself. Many
will prefer to hold that Acts has a wrong picture of the
events concerning the first visit of St. Paul to Jerusalem
after his conversion. II Cor. 11.32-33 is Paul's account of
his escape from Damascus. He says, 'In Damascus the
governor of Aretas the king kept the city of the Damascenes
with a garrison, desirous to apprehend me: And through a
window in a basket was I let down by the wall, and escaped
his hands.' Notice that the enmity came from the 'Ethnarch' (the real word which is translated GOVERNOR) of
Aretas, who reigned over the Nabataeans of Arabia from

9 B.C. to A.D. 40. In Acts the enmity comes from the Jewish community inside the city, not from an Arabian garrison outside its gates. Harmonization is not impossible —the Jews *might* have formed a plot with Aretas's ethnarch —but it is at least rather difficult. That Paul escaped from a window in the city wall of Damascus by an adventurous descent in a BASKET is assured, but exactly why he had to do this we shall never know.

(b) The nature of Saul's conversion

To us moderns, visions and auditions of supernatural events are things which cannot easily be believed in. We tend to put them down to hallucinations or delusions. That the ' mechanics ' of a vision such as that seen by Saul on the Damascus Road may be partially understood by psychological means is not impossible. What is certain is that Paul, and Luke too, felt no difficulties of this sort. The conversion undoubtedly took place, and however we try to explain it, we shall be unlikely to get much nearer to the actual events than we do when we accept the Acts story as basically true. It is possible, however, to make some guesses as to what had been going on in Paul's mind *before* this event. Paul was a pupil of Gamaliel (Acts 22.3), and possibly was affected by Gamaliel's hesitancy about attacking the Christians. But Paul was also a passionate supporter of the Jewish Law (see Phil. 3.4-6), and as such could not bring himself to believe that one who had fallen foul of the law, had in fact repeatedly defied it, could possibly be the Messiah. He was probably affected also by the selfless manner of Stephen's death. His journey to Damascus represented an effort to stifle his doubts by more vigorous activity. When he approached Damascus, he had to decide whether to embark on his second great wave of persecuting activity. The light came from heaven, and he entered Damascus as a virtual convert. The essence of the conversion experience was in hearing the words I AM JESUS. Jesus, then, was at

God's right hand, risen and exalted. He was also one with
His persecuted followers. Paul realized that he was wrong,
and submitted his whole life to the obedience of Christ. All
the stories stress the fact that with the conversion came the
call to be a missionary to the Gentiles, and this is the most
important sequel to the whole experience.

1. Continuation of 8.3.

2. The potential victims at Damascus were probably Christians who had fled from Jerusalem.

4. Saul, Saul
   He hears his name in its Hebrew, or Aramaic form.
'Paul' is not a Christian name, but the Grecized version of
'Saul'.

5. it is hard for thee, etc.
   Not in the true text here but is borrowed from the account
in Acts 26.14. **pricks** = goads, pointed sticks for guiding
oxen.

15. This verse describes in a sentence the career of Paul,
which Acts is to unfold.

16. he must suffer
   The Greek words are the same as those frequently used
in the Gospels about Jesus.

18. Baptism is considered the necessary means of entry into
the Church, and carries with it the gift of the Spirit.

20. he is the Son of God
   The phrase here means 'the Messiah'. (Cf. verse 22,
below, and Mark 14.62.)

24-25. Cf. II Cor. 11.32-33.

27. Barnabas has a distinct character in the New Testament stories.   He is usually a helper and encourager.

29. Paul's work is among the Hellenists, i.e.. the Greek-speaking Jews, as Stephen's had been.

30. Tarsus
Capital of Cilicia, in S.E. Asia Minor.   Cf. 21.39.   A University city, well known for its Stoic teachers.

31. the churches
The best MSS. have 'the church', which is interesting, as it is the first (and only) example in Acts of 'the church' as meaning the whole church of an area, as distinct from the several local churches which make it up.

VI

PETER AS A MISSIONARY TO THE GENTILES: FOUNDATION OF THE GENTILE CHURCH AT ANTIOCH
9.32–11.30

This section of the book is of particular importance, for it tells of the first conversions of Gentiles to the Christian faith. Hitherto we have read only of proselytes (apart from Jews) being baptized, but now the latent power of Christianity breaks through another shell, and the way is prepared for the great Gentile mission of St. Paul. It is noteworthy that the step of admitting the first Gentile (Cornelius) is taken by Peter, thus showing that (at least in the eyes of Luke) Peter equally with Paul stood solidly behind the Gentile mission (cf. Gal. 2.7-8). The great story of Cornelius (10.1–11.21) is preceded by the account of two miracles in the neighbourhood of Caesarea, and is followed by the story of how Gentiles were admitted to the faith in Antioch.

TWO MIRACLES OF PETER
9.32-43

Luke weaves together certain isolated items of tradition and makes a connected story of them. The first is the curing of Aeneas, at Lydda (32-35); then follows the raising of Tabitha or Dorcas from the dead. Both miracles were similar to miracles of Jesus (cf. the healing of the paralytic, Mark 2.1-12, and the raising of Jairus's daughter, Mark 5.22-43). Undoubtedly we are to see here the power of

Jesus Christ at work in His Church. In the case of Aeneas, Peter says plainly: JESUS CHRIST MAKETH THEE WHOLE (v. 34).

Before going further, we may insert a note on *Miracles*.

Our minds, conditioned by twentieth-century scientific assumptions, cannot read these stories without asking, 'Did they happen?' 'Are they true?' Let us make a few assertions, in order to get the whole matter into perspective. (1) Many miracles are recorded in the life of Jesus, less are recorded of the apostles, hardly any of the later Christian leaders, until we come to the clearly legendary miracles recorded of many medieval saints. (2) A non-scientific age would see a miracle where we might not, and would accept a miracle on slighter historical evidence than we should be prepared to do. (3) Evidently from the earliest Christian times there was a strong belief that both Jesus and His apostles *did* work miracles. (4) We must distinguish between two different questions that are often confused. (*a*) Can miracles happen? (*b*) Did any particular miracle happen? (*a*) is a philosophical question, and the answer is 'yes'. We are always learning, and the more we learn (e.g. of medical science) the less likely we are to say that anything is 'impossible'. (*b*) is a historical question, and we cannot help demanding exceptionally good evidence for very unusual events. Most scholars would sum up their views about biblical miracles like this: Miracles were from the earliest times part of the gospel tradition: individual miracle stories may have been exaggerated, or fancifully embellished: the event of the Incarnation was itself of such a unique character that extraordinary events might well accompany it, and apparently did so. Perhaps when the Church was more established it was possible for God's attestation of its message to take other forms.

32. Lydda
West of Jerusalem near the coast.

36. Joppa
Large port, near Lydda.

Dorcas
The name means 'gazelle', but whether this had any
relation to Dorcas's physical or personal qualities, we cannot say.

THE STORY OF CORNELIUS'
CONVERSION
10.1-48

This long story easily divides into sections (for which see
below), but we must first consider it as a whole. The great
point to grasp is that Cornelius was a Gentile, a Roman
soldier. He was a 'God-fearer', but not a full proselyte.
He therefore counted as a Gentile. He is told in a vision
to send for Peter from Joppa. Peter at Joppa almost at the
same time has a vision which leads him to accept Cornelius' request as a divine command. Peter goes to Cornelius, preaches the gospel to him, he receives the Holy
Spirit, whereupon Peter baptizes him. When Peter goes
back to Jerusalem he has to justify his action to the conservative section of the Jerusalem Church, the particular
charge being the fact that he had entered a Gentile house,
which was forbidden to strict Jews. He defends himself
by telling the whole story of both visions.

Now the important thing to ask is 'why does St. Luke
tell this story at such length?' 'What is he trying to impress
upon his readers?' Two things, primarily. (1) That the
admission of Gentiles was due to God's initiative. This is
the most important point, and the detailed study of the
narrative bears out the importance of it. Scholars consider
that the editorial work done by Luke on the original
tradition shows that his interest lies just here (see M.

Dibelius, ' The Conversion of Cornelius ', in *Studies in the
Acts of the Apostles*). (2) That Peter, as well as Paul, was on
the side of the admission of Gentiles. At some later time,
Peter reverted to a more conservative position, and refused
to eat with Gentile Christians at Antioch. (See Gal. 2.12.)
Possibly repercussions of this controversy between Paul and
Peter continued for some time, and Luke wanted to claim
Peter as an ally in his support of the liberal policy.

CORNELIUS' VISION
10.1-8

1. Caesarea
Administrative capital of Judaea.

Italian band
Cohort (600 men) from Italy.

2. This centurion (an officer with 100 men under him) is
similar in character to the centurion mentioned in St. Luke's
Gospel (Luke 7.4-5).

PETER'S VISION
10.9-16

Peter is prepared for the arrival of Cornelius' messengers
by a vision of his own, that of the sheet with unclean beasts
in it. In his trance, being already hungry (v. 10), Peter
dreams of food, and as often happens in dreams, it is a case
of ' so near and yet so far '. The food is there, but it is
forbidden food. Only certain animals were ' clean ' to the
Jew. (See Lev. 11 for the Laws.) The voice from heaven
tells him that he must not call common (unclean) what God
has cleansed. Possibly this anecdote originally had reference to the Antioch food dispute (referred to above).

15. We are reminded of Mark 7.19 (R.V.), 'This he said, making all meats clean.'

PETER VISITS CORNELIUS
10.17-33

The story runs on naturally. Peter responds to the call from Cornelius, and after travelling to Caesarea, a largely Gentile city, he enters the soldier's house (v. 27). This was a big step, as Peter shows in the next verse (v. 28).

PETER'S SPEECH TO CORNELIUS
AND HIS FRIENDS
10.34-43

This section gives us one of the clearest summaries of the apostolic *Kerygma* or message. The first three verses provide the link with the occasion. What Peter says is, in effect: I now see that the message which God gave to the children of Israel is for all. God is no respecter of persons —He has no favourites. In every nation He can recognize those who 'fear him', and who deserve the reward of further truth. He then summarizes the 'word' or 'message' which did in fact come to the children of Israel through the life of Jesus. In the next few verses we have a summary of the gospel, as, for instance, it is contained in the Gospel according to St. Luke. This story runs from the baptism (the birth narratives are introductory) through the healing ministry to the Crucifixion and Resurrection. Notice particularly these words:

41. Not to all the people, but unto witnesses chosen before of God. All could see Jesus die, but not all could see Him risen. The *impact* of the risen Christ upon the witnesses was an historical fact—the appearances could, as

it were, be dated. But the life of the Risen Christ was from
its commencement, lived on a supra-historical plane: it was
not governed by the ordinary rules of time and space. In
this sense belief in the Resurrection is always an act of faith.
St. Peter specially recalls the *meals* which the apostles had
shared with the Risen Jesus (e.g. those mentioned in Luke
24.30-31 and 41-43). Doubtless the early Christians felt a
real continuity between these meals and the Eucharists of
their ordinary church life. The final message of the address
is in these verses:

42-43, where St. Peter announces that the Jesus of the
gospel is the appointed Judge of the world. Remission
of sin can follow faith in Him.

36-37. The grammar is very awkward, and the text has
been varied to make it easier. 36 is a sentence that
never reached a logical conclusion, but its general meaning is clear enough.

THE HOLY SPIRIT GIVEN TO
GENTILES
10.44-48

Now the miracle happens, and on Cornelius and his
friends there breaks a new Pentecost. They begin to
SPEAK WITH TONGUES, as the first Christians had done at
Pentecost. St. Peter, feeling that if they had received the
Spirit they should have the sign of acceptance into the
Church, baptism, has them baptized. Notice how God
takes the initiative all through this story, even to the end.
The Spirit comes first: then baptism follows. Luke means
us to be in *no* doubt that God was behind the admission of
Gentiles: this is natural, for most of the rest of the book
is to be about this subject.

45. they of the circumcision

Those who believed that Jewish Law should prevail, and that the Church should be limited to the circumcised.

THE JERUSALEM CHURCH CONFIRMS PETER'S ACTION
11.1-21

It is clear that the Jerusalem Christians were very conservative. When Peter returned from Caesarea to Jerusalem the circumcision party taxed him with having entered a Gentile house and eaten with its occupants (v. 3). They do not fasten on the baptism of the Gentiles as the main crime, and curiously enough Peter does not refer to this matter in his defence. He just tells the whole story (Luke abbreviates it, for literary effect) and refers to the well-known saying of John the Baptist, to the effect that the Messiah would baptize not with water but with Holy Spirit. According to this account the Jerusalem Christians accepted the situation, saying, perhaps with a tinge of regret, ' Then hath God also to the Gentiles granted repentance unto life.' They continued to make difficulties, but these were on the terms on which Gentiles could be admitted to the Church, and on subsequent relations with them, rather than on the questions of admission itself (see Acts 15.1-28, and Gal. 2.11-14).

FIRST NEWS OF A CHURCH AT ANTIOCH
11.19-30

The chapter closes with news of the founding of a Gentile Church at Antioch, and of its first relations with the Church of Jerusalem. It makes a most suitable postscript to the

Cornelius story. We now know that the conversion of Gentiles is the will of God, and are ready to hear how it began to happen in a big way. Antioch was a very important city, right up in the north-east corner of the Mediterranean coast, a capital city, containing plenty of Jews, but a much greater number of Gentiles. It was to be the starting point of Paul's first missionary journey. Notice how it happened. There was a scattering of Greek-speaking Jewish Christians after the death of Stephen. Though these travelled far and wide—to Phenice, Cyprus, and Antioch (i.e. mainly northwards) they did not for the most part evangelize Gentiles (v. 19). But some of them did. Confronted with the great Greek city, they could not resist offering them the gospel too (v. 20). This was a momentous step. But (as we might have expected after the incident with Cornelius) THE HAND OF THE LORD WAS WITH THEM. A great number believed. Then the Jerusalem Church gets worried—for such is almost certainly the meaning of v. 22—but wisely sends as its emissary Barnabas, a man who has already shown his flexibility of mind by his reception of Saul (see 9.27). He was suitable for another reason too. He was from Cyprus (see 4.36), and this great step forward had been taken partly by Cypriots (v. 20). He was delighted with what he found, his only concern being that the conversion of the Gentiles should not turn out to be ephemeral (v. 23). He decides to fetch Saul from his native Tarsus, whither he had gone after his rather stormy days in Jerusalem after his conversion. Barnabas rightly selects him, a Greek-speaking Jew, coming from a University city, to train and guide the infant Antioch Church. Here the word CHRISTIAN is first used of Christ's followers.

The last verses of the chapter tell how a prophet named Agabus foretells a famine, and how this happened in the days of Claudius Caesar (about A.D. 44). Relief is sent to the churches of Judaea by Barnabas and Saul. This is the first news of an important matter in the apostolic Church.

the sending of help to Jerusalem from the Gentile churches
(see esp. Rom. 15.25-32, and other passages in the Epistles).
Besides the philanthropic motive, such gifts preserved the
sense of unity and solidarity between the new Gentile
churches and the original Hebrew nucleus in Jerusalem.

20. Grecians
Should be *Greeks*, which means Gentiles. They are
called Greeks, because since Alexander the Great's Empire,
Greek (or rather Hellenistic, late Greek) culture had spread
into all the cities of the Levant.

preaching the Lord Jesus
The Greek is *euaggelizomenoi ton kurion Iēsoun*: pro-
claiming the good news of the Lordship of Jesus. This was
just the point made by Peter in his speech to Cornelius:
HE IS LORD OF ALL. 'Jesus is the Lord' was the first Christian creed. (I Cor. 12.3.)

24. Luke means that had Barnabas not been **full of the
Holy Ghost,** he might not have been glad about the Gentile
mission.

25. Tarsus
Only some hundred miles away: Jerusalem was four
hundred.

26. Christians
The word is in Greek letters, made up like a Latin adjective, incorporating a Hebrew idea (Messiah, anointed). It
appears also in Acts 26.28 and I Peter 4.16. The use of the
new name indicates the emergence of the Church as a distinct entity—no longer just a branch of Judaism.

27. prophets
Christians who were thought to be able to express by

word or action, the mind of the Spirit of God. (See Acts 21.10-11 and I Cor. 12.28.)

28. great dearth throughout all the world

' All the world ' is something of an exaggeration, though there was widespread want under Claudius (Emperor, A.D. 41-54). Josephus tells of shortage of food A.D. 44-48.

30. This verse shows that the Jerusalem Church had **elders**, like the synagogues, the elders of which were called *zeqenim*. For the historical problems connected with this visit of Barnabas and Saul to Jerusalem, see notes on chapter 15.

VII

HEROD'S VAIN EFFORT TO CRUSH THE CHURCH
12

It is best to read this chapter as a whole, and to see it as an account of an unsuccessful effort to put down Christianity. The Herod of this chapter is Herod Agrippa I, nephew of the Herod before whom our Lord appeared in Luke 23.7-12. This Herod (Agrippa I) had had a chequered career, sometimes being quite out of favour at Rome, but just now his territory was extensive, covering more or less all Palestine. He was desperately anxious to please the Jews, as is plainly hinted in v. 3 of this chapter. Just as his uncle had been associated with the passion of Jesus, so this Herod plays his part, alongside the Jewish religious leaders, in harassing His followers. Thus James, one of our Lord's inner circle of disciples, is killed, and Herod imprisons Peter too, meaning to have him tried after the Passover. But it was in vain that 'the rulers took counsel' against Christ and His people. Peter is miraculously delivered from prison, and Herod himself comes to a painful death immediately after a great celebration in which he has been given divine honours. This celebration may have been held to celebrate Claudius's successful invasion of Britain, but there are other explanations of the festival, e.g. that it was a regular four-yearly festival, in honour of the Emperor, but also commemorating the founding of the city of Caesarea. The chapter reaches a climax in v. 24, THE WORD OF GOD GREW AND MULTIPLIED—another example of Luke's great principle that 'nothing can stop the gospel'.

ACTION AGAINST ST. JAMES AND
ST. PETER
12.1-19

2. We have no other information concerning the martyrdom of James, but it is of course prophesied by Jesus in Mark 10.39. Some have suggested that originally the tradition included also the death of John, but this rests on flimsy evidence.

4. quaternions
Groups of four soldiers.

Easter
The Passover.

5-19. Little comment is possible on the story of the miraculous escape of Peter. Though to many modern minds so difficult as to be more or less unbelievable, the story is told with great vividness, and gives a striking picture of the communal life of the primitive Church. Notice the first mention of John Mark, the probable author of Mark, in v. 12. And do not overlook that James (the other James, not the disciple, whose death has just been reported, but the brother of Jesus) is already a person of standing, to whom Peter's escape has to be reported (v. 17). We shall hear more of him later.

20-23. A strikingly similar account of Herod's death occurs in Josephus (*Antiquities* 19.8.2), though of course there are some differences.

20. The reconciliation of Tyre and Sidon seems to have been made to contribute to the glamour of the day.

21. a set day

March 5 or August 1, A.D. 44, have both been suggested for different reasons.

22-23. As so often in ancient literature, *nemesis* follows *hubris*. Self-glorification leads to disaster. *Eaten of worms* is a description given in ancient writings to humiliating and painful death. Josephus describes symptoms more suggestive of strangulated hernia.

24-25. Closing summary

Once more Luke sums up the whole passage by a general statement reminding us of his main theme—God's word continues to advance. Barnabas and Saul return to Antioch, and the stage is set for the next chapter, which describes the first great mission to the Gentiles.

VIII

THE FIRST GREAT GENTILE
MISSION
13–15

THE HOLY SPIRIT CALLS FOR A
NEW STEP FORWARD
13.1-3

Great importance attaches to the next two chapters, for they tell of the first extensive piece of evangelistic work undertaken by Paul, who is to be the central figure for the rest of the book. Moreover, although Paul (and his companion, Barnabas) usually began their work in any new city by preaching to Jews, it is on this tour that they begin to put Gentiles in the centre of the picture as the principal object of their evangelistic work. The start of the tour is therefore of special significance.

It starts from Antioch, the city in which the gospel had first been preached to Gentiles in considerable numbers (see 11.20), and the suggestion of v. 1 is that Antioch was particularly well supplied with ' prophets and teachers ', i.e. men who spoke under the guidance of the Holy Spirit, and men who had the gift of building up converts in the faith. Besides Barnabas and Saul, of whom we have heard already, three others are named, probably all Hellenist Jews, one of whom had been brought up with Herod the tetrarch. Luke is anxious to show people of aristocratic origin who support Christ's cause (see Luke 8.3, where Chuza, one of our Lord's women followers is said to be the wife of Herod's steward). The presence of the prophets and teachers was doubtless the human condition of receiving a new challenging message from God. This came AS THEY MINISTERED TO THE LORD, AND FASTED. While we cannot say precisely what this means, we shall be safe in assuming that it stands for some time of concentrated prayer and worship, possibly on the Lord's Day, accompanied by abstinence from food, either incidental to the long-continued prayer, or of a semi-liturgical character. At this time the Holy Spirit said (doubtless through the lips of one of the prophets named) SEPARATE ME BARNABAS AND SAUL FOR THE WORK WHERE-UNTO I HAVE CALLED THEM. This was one of the most important calls that have ever come to the Church. Luke means us to know that this new step was not self-imposed, but was part of a divine plan. After further prayer and abstinence, they laid hands on them (a sign of blessing and commission) and SENT THEM AWAY, probably not knowing at all where the divine leading was going to take them. Luke tells us (in v. 4) that it was through the ' sending forth ' of the Holy Spirit, that they arrived at Seleucia, the port for Antioch.

THE CYPRUS MISSION
13.4-13

Not unnaturally the missionaries stop at the first natural port of call, the island of Cyprus, about 100 miles south-west of Seleucia. They preached to Jews in the synagogues of Salamis, the important city on the east coast of the island, then made their way to Paphos, at the western end, the centre of the Roman government. Since 22 B.C. Cyprus had been a ' senatorial province ' (i.e. under the Senate, not directly under the Emperor), and such provinces were governed by Proconsuls (as Luke clearly knows: see v. 7, where A.V. has *deputy* translating *anthupatos*, pro-consul). Just as Simon Peter, on one of his early journeys was

troubled by a sorcerer, Simon Magus, so Paul is confronted
with a sorcerer bearing the sacred name of Bar-Jesus (son
of Jesus), also named Elymas. This sorcerer is at the court
of the pro-consul, Sergius Paulus (v. 7). This name is
known in first-century Roman history, but any identifica-
tions are precarious. What is interesting is that the very
first Roman governor whom Paul meets is favourably disposed (v. 7), and in spite of the opposition of Elymas,
believes (v. 12).

5. and they had also John to their minister

John Mark, who appears in 12.12, 25; 13.13; 15.37-39;
Col. 4.10; I Peter 5.13; II Tim. 4.11. His career makes an
interesting study. Nobody knows what sort of a ' servant '
he was, whether a practical assistant, or a ' servant of the
word ', i.e. some kind of a catechist. We also do not know
why John Mark left the party (see 13.13) and returned to
Jerusalem. Perhaps when he saw that the apostles were
going to approach Gentiles in a big way he hesitated, and
if this is so it might fit in with the difference which arose
later between Paul and Barnabas (see Gal. 2.13). Barnabas
was uncle to Mark, and the family may have taken a midway position between Jerusalem Christianity (' Jews first:
Gentiles only if they fit in with Jewish ideas ') and Pauline
Christianity (' There is no difference, but the same Lord is
rich unto all that call upon him '). But at present Barnabas
is one with Paul in his pro-Gentile attitude.

9. Saul (who also is called Paul)

Not Hebrew and Christian, but Hebrew and Greek.

9. Note that Paul's condemnation of Elymas takes place
when Paul is full of the Holy Spirit.

THE SECOND ANTIOCH, THE SCENE
OF A SECOND STEP FORWARD
13.14-48

The party crosses over to Asia Minor, and after an apparently short stay at Perga (see map), Paul and Barnabas go right up to Pisidian Antioch, i.e., to the middle of Phrygia-Galatia, that part of the large province of Galatia which included Phrygia (Antioch was not actually *in* Pisidia, only near it, as the best texts in Greek make clear). John Mark returned from Perga to Jerusalem, but the rest went up over the mountains, possibly to escape rapidly from the malarial coastlands.

At Antioch Paul accepts the invitation from the rulers of the synagogue to offer a WORD OF EXHORTATION, and 16-41 contain the substance of his address. In many ways it runs parallel to the apostolic proclamations of Peter, but there are some special features as we shall see. The passage should first be read through as a connected whole, and then the detailed points noted below can be examined.

16. ye that fear God
The 'God-fearers' were Gentiles who were attracted by Judaism, but who had not taken the step of circumcision. They were a fruitful field for evangelism. Perhaps Theophilus was one.

17-22. These verses sketch the history of the Jewish people from the Exodus to the time of David, something after the manner of the historical Psalms (e.g. Pss. 105, 106). When Paul reaches David the thought is transferred to Jesus, 'great David's greater son'.

23. Luke, like Matthew and Paul, already knows the tradition that Jesus comes from the historic line of David.

24-25. Luke never loses a chance to show how the work of John the Baptist heralded the days of the Messiah.

26-37. This passage follows the classical type of apostolic proclamation, dealing with the Jews' rejection of Christ, and God's reversal of man's verdict. The call to repentance follows.

38-39. The stress on forgiveness of sins, justification by faith, and the comparison between the gospel and the law are points which we should expect to appear in a sermon by the author of Romans. This passage is one of those which suggest that Luke had real knowledge of the kind of thing which Paul could be expected to say.

41. This verse seems to contain a condemnation of Paul's Jewish hearers before they have given their verdict, rather in the style of Stephen's fighting speech in chapter 7. The quotation is from Hab. 1.5.

42-43. These verses appear slightly contradictory. In v. 42 there is a contrast drawn between the Jews and the Gentiles, and this is the true preparation for what is coming in v. 46, but in v. 43 Jews as well as **religious proselytes** (another rather strange expression) show interest, and are considered by Paul and Barnabas to be **in the grace of God**, which presumably means that they actually believed.

45. The next week sees a great concourse gathered to hear the gospel, which provokes violent hostility from the Jews, probably based on jealousy.

46. A turning point in the story. Paul and Barnabas here lay down the thesis that the Jews have only themselves to blame for losing the great opportunity of obeying the gospel.

Ye put it from you
This leads to the momentous declaration **Lo, we turn to**

the Gentiles. The apostles quote in support Isa. 49.6, words
which are echoed in Simeon's Song (see Luke 2.32).

48 records the joy of the Gentiles at the good news and the
new opportunity which has come to them. Notice the
phrase: **and as many as were ordained to eternal life believed.** This indicates a doctrine of *predestination* in the
writer of Acts (cf. Rom. 8.29-30). The impression Luke
wants to make all the time is that a great plan of God is
being irrevocably unfolded. Antioch in Syria was the scene
of the first preaching of the gospel to Gentiles (Acts 11.20).
Antioch, near Pisidia, is the scene of the deliberate change-
over of Paul and Barnabas from being primarily preachers
to Jews to being primarily preachers to Gentiles.

A SUMMARY: PROGRESS AND
TROUBLE
13.49-52

The chapter ends with a typical Lucan summary, possibly
inserted by Luke to bridge the gap between one section or
story in his sources and the next. Note the main points.
(*a*) widespread preaching of the gospel (v. 49). (*b*) opposition from Jews (v. 50). (*c*) symbolic demonstration of the
responsibility of the hearers for rejection of the message (cf.
Mark 6.11). (*d*) joy, and a sense of possession by the Holy
Spirit, in the converts.

A MIXED RECEPTION IN ICONIUM
14.1-7

The missionaries make their way, in a south-south-
easterly direction to Iconium, in Lycaonia, which was now
part of the large province of Galatia, stretching in a belt

almost from the top to the bottom of what we call Asia
Minor. The paragraph does not run quite smoothly (e.g.
v. 3, with its 'therefore' hardly seems a natural sequel to
v. 2), but the general picture is clear enough. There was a
good response from both Jews and Greeks (v. 1). Hostile
Jews however enlisted the services of Gentiles against the
apostles (v. 2), the division between those in favour and
those against became acute (v. 4), and in the end there was
an assault, the attackers being made up of Gentiles, and of
Jews, the latter being led by their own rulers. News reached
the apostles in time, and they moved on quickly to another
area, going on in the same general south-easterly direction,
where were two more cities, Lystra and Derbe.

PAUL'S TURN TO HEAL AN
IMPOTENT MAN
14.8-18

One of the basic elements in the pattern of Acts is the
repetition, or echoing, in the life of St. Paul of things that
have happened to St. Peter. This may be a literary feature,
whereby Luke imports a kind of rhythm to his story, or he
may be keen to show that St. Paul really was a figure of equal
stature to St. Peter. When we remember that at Corinth, at
least, there was a 'Peter party' and a 'Paul party', it becomes possible that Luke wanted to do all he could to keep
St. Paul's reputation high. Certainly the parallel between
this story of the lame man at Lystra and the story of St.
Peter's lame man (3.1-11ff.) is very close. The little detail
STEDFASTLY BEHOLDING HIM in v. 9 is the same phrase
in the Greek as that translated FASTENING HIS EYES ON
HIM in 3.4 (*atenisas* followed by *autō* in this passage, by
eis auton in 3.4). In both cases the miracle has a remarkable effect on the eyewitnesses, so that St. Peter has to
show that it is not the *apostles'* power which has been at

work, but that of Christ, and St. Paul has to restrain the
crowds from worshipping him and Barnabas. 15-17 are
important (see below) as illustrating the kind of preaching which was addressed to pagans in the more outlying
areas.

11. speech of Lycaonia

The local language, of which little is now known.

12. Jupiter, Mercurius

The A.V. uses the Latin names for the chief of the gods
and for his son, the messenger of the gods. The Greek
original speaks of Zeus and Hermes. Possibly the local
inhabitants were worshipping traditional gods under the
Greek names. The story strongly suggests that Paul was
much younger than Barnabas.

13. The English of A.V. is not quite clear. For **the priest
of Jupiter, which was before their city** read *the priest of the
Temple of Jupiter which stood in the forefront of the
city.*

14. Paul and Barnabas were strong monotheists, and were
horrified at the idea of being worshipped.

15-17. Notice particularly the points in this little speech.
Their message, say the apostles, is a call to turn from
vanities to the living God. This is exactly what St. Paul
says his message was when he writes to the Thessalonians
(I Thess. 1.9-10. *Ye turned to God from idols to serve the
living and true God*). The true God was the creator of the
world (v. 15); His attitude to mankind in the past had been
one of patient acceptance of their errors (cf. Acts 17.30;
Rom. 1.28; 3.25 Gk.); the beneficent aspects of nature were
a witness to His power and goodness (cf. Romans 1.19-20).

THE RETURN JOURNEY
14.19-28

The last part of this chapter describes one new mission, that to Derbe, which follows a serious stoning of Paul at Lystra, after which the apostles make their way back, boldly visiting Lystra, Iconium, and Pisidian Antioch once more, then making their way to the coast at Attalia, and thence returning direct to Antioch in Syria, from whence they had set out. The little section contains some important information about the way in which the primitive Church was governed, while the closing verses repeatedly stress that the initiative in this first Gentile mission was God's and not man's. See 26, 27. They had been RECOMMENDED TO THE GRACE OF GOD at the outset; they came back to say what GOD HAD DONE; how He had opened the door of faith to Gentiles. It is a splendid preparation for the next chapter, which is to show with what difficulty the reception of Gentiles was really accepted by the Jewish Church.

19-20. The stoning of Paul. Referred to in II Cor. 11.25. Also possibly in Gal. 6.17.

22. This verse shows the pastoral care of the new Churches exercised by St. Paul. **Confirming** means strengthening. The whole of this verse is in line with Paul's teaching in I Thessalonians, see especially I Thess. 3.4.

23. The **elders** appointed were on the model of the Jewish *zeqenim* (=elders), who ruled in the affairs of the synagogues. We often read of them in the Gospels. Theirs would be the task of guiding and leading the churches once the apostles had left, but it is clear that their original appointment (the word *ordained* does not truly represent the Greek) was due to the apostles. Prayer and fasting is in this case connected more with the commendation of the Church to God than with the appointment of elders, but we cannot help noticing that the original commission to Paul and Barnabas (12.2) was accompanied by similar acts of religious devotion.

28. This verse suggests that the trouble of which we are to read in chapter 15 did not arise immediately.

IX

AGREEMENT ON THE TERMS OF GENTILE ADMISSION
15.1-35

We now come to one of the most interesting and important stories given us in Acts, that of the Jerusalem Council. One question had better be disposed of as soon as possible, the relation of this visit to the consultations between Paul and the Jerusalem leaders mentioned in Gal. 1.15-24 and 2.1-17. In Galatians, which we must remember is a first-hand authority in a way which Acts is not, we read of two visits of Paul, after his conversion, to Jerusalem. One (Gal. 1.18) took place three years after his conversion, the other (Gal. 2.1) fourteen years after the conversion (it is usual to make the fourteen years *include* the previous three). If we equate these two visits with the first two post-conversion visits in Acts, Gal. 1.18 must be described in Acts 9.26ff., and Gal. 2.1ff. in Acts 11.30. This would mean that the Jerusalem Council of Acts 15 is not described in Galatians for the very good reason that it had not happened when Galatians was written. But this means that Galatians has to be put as a very early Epistle, indeed the earliest of all, and not all scholars are able to accept this. If we identify Gal. 2.1ff. with Acts 15, as J. B. Lightfoot and many scholars have done, we have to assume either that Paul omitted any reference to one of his two earlier visits in Acts (in spite of particularly strong emphasis on his accuracy— see Gal. 1.20) or that Acts is wrong in recording these three visits—there would be only two altogether up to the time of the Jerusalem Council. Scholars like Lightfoot have held that the circumstances described in Acts 15 are so similar to those envisaged in Gal. 2 that the incidents referred to must be identical. But in his day it was usual to assume that Galatians was addressed to inhabitants of the old Kingdom of Galatia, in the north of Asia Minor. As Paul had not yet visited that part—and possibly never did so—that was an additional reason for accepting a later date for Galatians, and hence finding in it a description of the Jerusalem Council. Nowadays it is usual to see in the 'Galatians' inhabitants of a larger area, the Roman Province of Galatia. This came farther south, and included places like Lystra and Derbe. Galatians might therefore be addressed to those churches at any time after the first missionary journey.

It must be mentioned that serious scholars do not consider themselves bound to a strict *either/or* in this matter. There are other possible solutions. One is that the Jerusalem visits of Acts 11 and Acts 15 are alternate accounts of the same visit, wrongly separated by Luke. Some think that the missionary journey described in Acts 13 and 14 is really identical with that described in Acts in chapter 16. It is impossible to reach finality when so many various views are defended. To equate Acts 11 with Gal. 2 is the *simplest* solution, and the easiest to remember which is not unimportant. But anything like dogmatism is quite out of the question.

Once we have ceased to worry about strict chronology, we can give our attention to the general situation which led to the events of Acts 15. We have seen already that the Jerusalem Church was rather conservative in its attitude to Gentile converts. Peter had to take special steps to convince them that it was right to admit Cornelius. Antioch, however, was the centre of the Gentile mission. What more natural than that Jerusalem should send representatives to Antioch to investigate, and if possible set limits to the

admission of Gentiles? This was done (according to Acts
15.1). Galatians 2.12 says that 'certain came from James',
meaning James, the Lord's brother who was tender to the
conservative section (see Acts 21.18-20), showing (if our
identification of Acts 11 with Gal. 2 is correct) that such
interference happened more than once. These emissaries
(Acts 15) insisted that Gentile converts should be circumcised, and keep the Jewish Law. Apart from the brake
which such a rule would have put on the movement of
evangelism, it would have turned Christianity into a Jewish
sect, and made it very difficult for it to survive the fall of
Jerusalem in A.D. 70. And Acts is anxious to show that the
Gentile mission is something which *God* has undertaken,
and imposed upon the Church, and that it is not for the
Church to set artificial limits to the movements of the
Spirit. Hence the strong opposition to such restrictions
from Paul and Barnabas. The Church then 'arranged' for
Paul and Barnabas, with others, to visit the apostles and
elders about the question. (According to the Western text
—for information on this text see note at end of book—
they, i.e. the emissaries, *ordered* Paul and Barnabas to go.
If this text is correct, the Jerusalem Church still had strong
authoritative powers over daughter Churches. This is possible, but the new movement was already striking out on its
own.)

The Conference, according to Acts, was amicable. There
was some difficulty with some ex-Pharisee Christians (see
v. 5), but the four chief speakers, Peter, Paul, Barnabas
and even James, are in general agreement that circumcision
might not be imposed. Peter starts from the fact that he
had brought in the first Gentile, Cornelius, under the direct
inspiration of God. (Now we can see why Luke underlined
that incident so strongly.) Barnabas and Paul lay stress on
the miracles which have taken place, as evidence of God's
co-operation in the mission. James, who seems to be a
sort of chairman, agrees, and gives as the verdict of the

Council the decision that no other burdens are to be laid
on the Gentiles than certain 'necessary things'. What
these were we must discuss, but they did not include circumcision. They concerned the conditions under which Jewish
and Gentile Christians could live together in one community. This also was a delicate question and at one time
(Gal. 2) Peter, and even Barnabas, had been more cautious
than Paul thought right.

The exact meaning of the NECESSARY THINGS (Acts 15.20,
29) must be considered. One of the difficulties is that it
is not easy to say just what was the original form of the
vital verse (v. 20). The text in the A.V. (which is that, in
this passage, of the group of manuscripts usually most
trusted, the so-called Alexandrian text) lists four things to be
avoided—POLLUTIONS OF IDOLS (i.e. food previously offered
in sacrifice to idols), FORNICATION, THINGS STRANGLED (i.e.
meat not killed in the Jewish way, not 'kosher' meat) and
BLOOD (i.e. the same kind of food referred to in the previous
phrase, meat with the blood in it). The so-called Western
text (see appendix on this subject) omits 'things strangled',
but adds 'and not to do to others things that they do not
wish done to themselves', the negative form of the 'Golden
Rule' of Matt. 7.12. An early manuscript recently dis-
covered (P. 45) omits 'fornication' from the list as given in
our Bibles. Now without going into all the details, it can
be said that in all probability the original text had only *two*
prohibitions, pollutions of idols and 'blood', i.e. it was a
simple food rule, stating that Gentiles must respect the
traditional rules of food operating in the Jewish community, if they wished to have fellowship with them. The
later additions marked a tendency to add rules governing
moral behaviour as well.

Questions have been asked as to whether Acts can be
right in stating that these rules (even in their brief form)
were definitely laid down as Acts say they were. It is
certainly strange that St. Paul never refers to the rules in

his letters, and often they would have been very relevant to his purpose (e.g. when discussing food offered to idols in I Cor. 8). But it is dangerous to argue from silence. It can be said that the *spirit* of his teaching, that of mutual consideration, is the *spirit* of the Jerusalem Council. And there is some evidence that the Jerusalem rules were widely known in the early Christian world. (See Rev. 2.14, 20, and Eusebius, *Ecc. Hist.* v. 1, 26.)

Whatever may have been the original facts, St. Luke is quite clear in the value he attaches to the story. For him, it marks the end of doubt and difficulty in the reception of the Gentiles. It is the natural conclusion of a movement beginning with the conversion of Cornelius, and foreshadowed by the words of the Risen Lord in 1.8.

1. Cf. Gal. 2.12 'certain came from James'. Even if this passage in Galatians describes a different incident from that referred to in Acts 15.1, it shows that the Jerusalem Church, or some of its members, were concerned to slow down the pro-Gentile policy of the Antioch Church. The whole Epistle to the Galatians shows that Judaising emissaries were also at work in the more outlying Churches, e.g. those of Lystra and Derbe.

2. they determined that Paul and Barnabas, and certain other of them, should go up to Jerusalem unto the apostles and elders about this question

Who are meant by *they*? The Western text is so worded that, according to this text, it was those who came from Judaea who 'ordered' Paul and Barnabas to go up to Jerusalem. The usual text is ambiguous, and *they* could be THE BRETHREN of v. 1. In any case the word **determined** (=arranged) is less strong than the word in the Western text, which is *ordered*. It is unfortunate that a textual difficulty should occur just here, because on the interpretation of this passage turns the question as to how much actual control of daughter Churches was exercised by the mother Church of Jerusalem.

apostles and elders

We do not know how many apostles were left in Jerusalem by this time. James (the brother of John) was dead. Peter was certainly not always there, but was present at the Conference. James the brother of our Lord was probably counted as an apostle. The elders would be senior and trusted leaders of the community.

3-5. Luke shows that opposition to reception of Gentiles was not found in Phenice and Samaria, and only on the part of certain ex-Pharisees at Jerusalem.

6. This verse says that the apostles and elders came together to discuss the question, but v. 12 refers to ALL THE MULTI-TUDE, and v. 22 to THE WHOLE CHURCH. The natural explanation is that the general body of Christians were also present or rather represented, for there were too many to be present all at once.

7-11. Peter bases everything on his experiences with Cornelius, showing what importance Luke meant us to attach to that story. V. 11 might have been spoken by Paul himself. We shall never know for certain whether the incident at Antioch, when Peter took a more conservative line, happened after or before this speech at the Council.

12. Luke does not give the details of the speeches of Barnabas and Paul, because they obviously consisted of the stories in chapters 13 and 14. But the fact that he assumes knowledge of those stories shows that his actual *account* of the Conference was a literary compilation, intended for readers of Acts, not a transcript of any sort of 'minutes'.

13. James says the final word. By this time he was the acknowledged leader of the Jerusalem Church. St. Paul says that he was given a vision of the Risen Lord (I Cor. 15.7). He apparently achieved a position of respect even among ordinary Jews (see Eusebius, *Ecc. Hist.* ii. 23, and Josephus, *Antiquities* 20.9.1).

14. Simeon

James uses a form of Peter's first name which is closer to the Hebrew than the usual Greek form, transliterated as *Simon*.

16-17. There is a problem here. The verses which James quotes (Amos 9.11-12) are quoted from the *Greek* O.T., the LXX, and do not make a suitable 'missionary' quotation in the Hebrew (for which, see English of R.V. of Amos). This suggests that the actual speech of James must be largely a later composition, for it seems most unlikely that James would have used the Septuagint. But if the whole assembly contained many Greek-speaking Christians, perhaps that cannot be entirely ruled out.

19. my sentence is

James seems to sum up the debate, and to formulate the decision.

20. See general note above.

21. A very obscure verse, often taken in one of two opposite senses. (1) 'Every city has its instructed Jews, so some respect for Jewish rules will always be necessary.' (2) 'Moses has plenty of advocates for *his* law of circumcision, so we need not worry about that.' The first is preferable.

22. The final action taken (the sending of the letters) was agreed by apostles, elders, and the whole Church.

23. Curious that the letter is not addressed to communities beyond Cilicia, the first province ' round the corner ' of the southern coast of Asia Minor.

24. subverting your souls
The action of the emissaries is wholeheartedly repudiated.

27. Judas and Silas are sent as well as Barnabas and Paul, as the evidence of the latter two might not have been sufficient, as they were clearly interested parties.

28. it seemed good to the Holy Ghost and to us
One of the strongest indications that the early Christians felt the presence, activity and authority of the Holy Spirit in and through their corporate actions (cf. 5.39; 13.2; 20.23).

X

ANOTHER GREAT SWEEP
FORWARD
15.36–20.38

The way has now been cleared for still more extensive
missionary work. This begins with a suggestion of Paul to
Barnabas that they revisit the scenes of their earlier missionary successes, in Cyprus and Asia Minor. A difference
arises between Barnabas and Paul (see below), and as a
result Barnabas goes to Cyprus, and Paul (with Silas) goes
overland through Cilicia to Lystra and Derbe. The further
course of this important journey will appear below, but we
must note at once that it was to be extended to the important centres of Philippi, Thessalonica, Athens, Corinth,
and it also included a brief stay at Ephesus. Many of the
communities founded in this journey afterwards become the
recipients of letters from St. Paul now found in the New
Testament (Philippians, I and II Thessalonians, I and II
Corinthians and possibly Ephesians), so we can supplement
what we know from Acts of Paul's work among them with
what can be deduced from the letters. It may be said
therefore that we know more of this section of the apostolic
history than of any other period in the first century.
Throughout there is a strong sense of the guidance and
initiative of the Holy Spirit, and the subsequent history of
the Church shows how vital for the development of Christianity was the building up of these Churches round the
Aegean Sea. Greek remained the official language of the
Christian Church for another two hundred years or so, even

at Rome, and this shows what formative influence was
extended from these Churches throughout the Christian
world.

BARNABAS AND PAUL SEPARATE
15.36-41

This section describes a difference between the two
great companions of the first journey, Barnabas and Paul.
According to Acts, it arose on the question as to whether
they should take John Mark, Barnabas's nephew, with them
a second time.   Paul thought not; he could not overlook
Mark's defection half-way through the first journey (13.13).
Barnabas, perhaps influenced by family feeling, wanted to
take him again.   It may be that behind the personal question
there lay some difference of approach.   Certainly we know
from Gal. 2.13 that at one time Barnabas gave way to
Judaising pressure in the matter of eating with Gentiles.
Eventually, Barnabas set off with Mark alone to Cyprus,
and Paul took Silas, one of those who had come to Antioch
with him and Barnabas, from Jerusalem, bearing the
apostolic letter.   Paul (and Acts from now on has little to
say of any other mission than that of Paul) goes north,
through the mountain pass known as the Cilician Gates, on
his way to Derbe and Lystra (v. 41).

HOW THE GOSPEL REACHED
MACEDONIA
16.1-12

As Paul was approaching his previous field of labour
from the opposite direction he reached the farthest extremity of his first journey at almost the beginning of this
one, so we find him, in 16.1, already at Derbe and Lystra

(note the order). In one of these towns he found Timothy
(see below), who from then on becomes one of Paul's important companions. As Timothy had one Jewish parent,
Paul gave him the sign of circumcision before taking him
as one of his helpers. He did not want Gentiles to be
circumcised, but he did not object to Jews receiving the
traditional mark of the Covenant, and it would have been
unnecessarily provocative to have as companion an uncir-
cumcised Jew. (Cf. I Cor. 9.20, ' Unto the Jews I became
as a Jew that I might gain the Jews.')

There is some difficulty in tracing out on the map the
exact course of Paul's journey over Asia Minor. The
difficult verses are 6 and 7. Study them carefully. They
state three facts. (a) They passed through Phrygia and the
region of Galatia. (b) They could not preach in Asia.
(c) They tried in vain to enter Bithynia. If you consult the
map, you will see that the *general* direction of their course
is clear. They were going north-west over Asia Minor, and
this fits in with their ultimate destination, Troas (v. 8),
in the extreme north-west corner. The details are more
doubtful. The first statement (they passed through Phrygia,
etc.) is particularly difficult. The Greek is *tēn Phrugian kai
Galatikēn chōran*. This can be translated ' Phrygia and the
Galatian region ', or (more easily) ' the Phrygian and Galatian
region '. Almost everybody agrees that whatever ' Galatian
region ' means, it does not mean the old Kingdom of Galatia
in the north of Asia Minor. The most acceptable view is
that it means ' Phrygia Galatica ', i.e. that part of Phrygia
which lay in the large province of Galatia. But this view
is not free from difficulties (see B.C., Vol. V, pp. 224ff., *Paul's
route in Asia Minor*). Then we are told that they were forbidden by the Holy Ghost to preach the word in Asia. This
means the large area covering all the western end of Asia
Minor, the Roman province of ' Asia '. It does not say that
they could not *enter* Asia, indeed Troas, their final point, is
in Asia. Then, when they reached Mysia, the area in the

north-west of Asia, they tried to turn north-east into
Bithynia, but this proved impossible.

Without going further into the complicated historical and
geographical questions involved, we must notice the *religious*
purpose of this section.   Luke means to bring his heroes to
Troas by the direct guidance of the Spirit, so that they are
ready for the vision of the young man of Macedonia (across
the Aegean Sea) calling for help.   What is really happening
in this section is that Luke is preparing for the next step,
the crossing of the water to what we now call Greece.

4. According to Acts, Paul and Silas were loyal propagators
of the apostolic decrees.

9. This is the signal for a great step forward, as a result of
which the gospel is brought to Europe.

10. we endeavoured
The first 'we passage'.   Perhaps Luke belonged to
Philippi, and was visiting Troas at the time.   Note the stress
on the Lord's call, completing the impression made in the
previous verses, that the apostles are following a divine
plan.

12. the chief city of that part of Macedonia
'A leading city, etc.' or 'a city of the first part of Macedonia'.

a colony
A city for Roman settlers, with special rights.

PAUL AND SILAS AT PHILIPPI
16.13-40

13-15. The apostles go to a place of prayer (in effect, a
synagogue) and either sit inside or outside.   They get an

opportunity to speak to the women worshippers. A proselyte woman, from Thyatira, accepts the gospel, is baptized,
and entertains the travelling missionaries.

16-18. A demon-possessed girl is cured.

16. spirit of divination
Lit. 'a Python spirit', a ventriloquist, or person who gave
vent to oracular utterances.

19-40. Arrest and escape: A gaoler converted. The loss
of gain leads to hostility from the girl's employers, and they
drag Paul and Silas to the rulers (*archontes*).

19-20. Probably **rulers** and **magistrates** are the same people,
the praetors or *duum viri*.

23. The missionaries receive the first official punishment of
which we have knowledge. (See II Cor. 11.25.)

25-40. This vivid story can best be discussed as a whole. It
is a striking example of the principle which we have seen
dominates the book, 'Nothing can stop the gospel'. Here
was a situation in which indeed it might seem to have been
effectively stopped. Its representatives were beaten, imprisoned (in the *inner* prison) and firmly fastened in the
stocks. Even in this situation, and at the depressing hour
of midnight, their faith and confidence were such that they
were able to pray and praise, and this not secretly. At this
point came the earthquake, which Luke certainly intends us
to take as a direct intervention of Providence. In the con-
fusion which follows, the gaoler, now afraid because of the
probable escape of his charges, is found on his knees before
Paul and Silas, saying SIRS, WHAT MUST I DO TO BE SAVED?
He had come to feel that they stood for a supernatural
power, which had shown its displeasure at their imprison-

ment by the earthquake. Whatever limited meaning he attached to the word 'saved', the apostles took him at his word, and replied, in a sentence which sums up the whole message of the New Testament, BELIEVE ON THE LORD JESUS CHRIST, AND THOU SHALT BE SAVED, AND THY HOUSE. A Gentile gaoler could not be expected to make much of this, but v. 32 says that THEY SPAKE UNTO HIM THE WORD OF THE LORD, doubtless showing who Jesus was, and how all men could put their trust in Him. He accepts the message, showing his acceptance first by the practical step of tending the wounds he had caused, then by baptism (shared, according to current ideas of family solidarity, by all his house), then by a common meal (had this a rudimentary Eucharistic character?). In the morning (v. 35) the magistrates send the SERGEANTS (lit. *lictors*, attendants on the magistrates, carrying a bundle of rods as symbol of their office) with an order for the release of Paul and Silas. The latter reject this indirect message, and insist on the personal word of the magistrates, claiming to have been wrongly flogged, being ROMANS. Apparently Silas shared Paul's citizenship (cf. 22.25ff.). Citizens were immune from flogging. The magistrates come, and ask them to leave the city. Even this the apostles do at their leisure, first paying a friendly call on Lydia, and giving a message of cheer to the brethren. This must have been a most unexpected turn of events for them. Perhaps Luke has his eye on Theophilus in this story. Among other things it says, ' Magistrates who ill-treat Christians regret it in the end '.

THE ROUTE TO ATHENS
17.1-15

The missionaries now make their way along a well-established route (the Via Ignatia) to Thessalonica (the Salonika of the first World War) the capital of Macedonia.

Here Paul devotes three sabbaths to reasoning with the Jews in their synagogue. Notice the three points of the message addressed to Jews, as given in v. 3. (1) Christ's death was according to God's plan. (2) He had risen from the dead. (3) He was the Messiah. The quick response of a good number led to violent objections from the non-responsive Jews, and they assaulted the house of Jason, where (see v. 7) the missionaries had been received. The missionaries were not there at the time, but they managed to get Jason and some other Christians and brought them before THE RULERS OF THE CITY (v. 6, lit. politarchs, this name being confirmed by many inscriptions as the right one for the official heads of Thessalonica). They charged them with actions subversive of Caesar's rule (v. 7). Though somewhat disturbed, the politarchs took no serious action, only taking security from Jason and his friends.

It is clearly no place for Paul and Silas, so they move on, south-west, to Beroea. Here there is an intelligent response to the teaching from the Old Testament (v. 11), but Jews from Thessalonica pursue them, and begin stirring up more trouble. Paul is taken on, apparently alone, to Athens, a city too big to make Jewish riots a great danger. Silas and Timothy stay behind (see note v. 14). So Paul arrives at the great intellectual centre of ancient times.

It is interesting that Acts begins in Jerusalem, the centre of the greatest religious community of the ancient world, and ends in Rome, the political centre. Half-way through Paul preaches in Athens. Thus the message of Christ is preached in the centres of Hebrew, Greek and Latin culture.

3. The same theme as our Lord developed on the Emmaus journey according to Luke 24.

5. lewd fellows of the baser sort

It is a pity to part with this picturesque phrase from the

A.V., but the R.V. 'certain vile fellows of the rabble' is better, the literal meaning being 'certain evil men of those frequenting the market-place'.

the people
    Lit. the *dēmos*, the citizen body.

6. these that have turned the world upside down
    This was an exaggeration at the time, but it was to be true enough in the course of a few centuries.

14. According to this passage (and 18.5) Silas and Timothy stayed at Beroea, but were rapidly summoned to Athens (v. 15). In 18.5, they arrive, not at Athens, which city Paul has already left, but at Corinth, his next stopping place. I Thess. 3.1ff. says that Paul faced solitude at Athens, by sending Timothy to Thessalonica, who returned to Paul with good news of the Church there (I Thess. 3.6). If this return is to be equated with the arrival of Timothy and Silas in Acts 18.5, we must presume (1) that Timothy's visit to Thessalonica took place after his rejoining of Paul (cf. Acts 17.15), (2) that Silas was also dispatched on a visit to ' somewhere in Macedonia ', possibly Philippi.

PAUL AT ATHENS
17.16-34

These nineteen verses contain some of the most interesting material in the whole of the New Testament. Needless to say, they have given rise to endless discussion, for, in addition to the many exciting topics raised by the story itself, it so happens that there are a number of points where the exact meaning is not quite clear, and scholars have been discussing them for centuries, and will doubtless go on doing so.

We deal first of all with the broad issues which arise, then, in the notes, with the detailed points.

The situation envisaged in the story is one of unique interest. Paul here confronts the serried ranks of Greek culture and philosophy. Athens no longer could boast great names like those of Plato and Aristotle, but something of the aura of the great days still hung over the beautiful city, and it was still a centre of lively academic discussion. It was to a representative audience of philosophically-minded listeners that Paul had to proclaim the gospel of salvation through faith in a crucified but risen Jewish Messiah.

Verses 16-21 set the stage, and problems arising in this section are discussed below. 22-31 give the famous speech, and 32-34 the result. The speech is unlike anything else in Acts in that it makes use of ideas, and even quotations culled from the common stock-in-trade of Hellenistic writers. Paul takes his start from an altar inscribed ' To an unknown God ' (v. 23: for the problem, see below) and goes on to preach from this text a sermon against idolatry, a sermon which shows how in all men there is something implanted by God, which in its turn is intended to lead men back to God. God, according to Paul in this speech, has overlooked THE TIMES OF THIS IGNORANCE (during which man has given himself to idols) but now calls on all men to repent, in preparation for the final judgment, which has been committed to the Risen Christ.

Some scholars (e.g. the great German scholar, Martin Dibelius) hold that the Paul of the Epistles could never have gone so far in establishing common ground between himself and the Hellenistic pagan world, and that the sermon is therefore without historical foundation, except as a relic of the apologetic addressed to cultivated pagans at the time when Acts was written (rather late, according to Dibelius). Against this view, notice two points. (1) Paul shows no mercy to idolatry, but does appeal to the more lofty type of Stoic thought as an indication to his hearers that even their own thinkers show how wrong their current practice is. (2) Paul does show in Romans 1.20-21, and 2.14-16, that the Gentiles are not without any knowledge of God, and that they have enough light to make them responsible before God in the day of judgment.

It is commonly said that the mission at Athens was a failure, and that Paul's repudiation of 'the wisdom of this world' in I Cor. 1 and 2 is intended to mark his rejection of any further efforts of this sort. Such a view is rather naïve. In any case, is it true that the Athens speech was a failure? There were, according to v. 34, some who believed, including a member of the Areopagus, and a woman named Damaris, probably of some standing, as well as others. There were also some who expressed a desire to hear more (v. 32). It has been said that if a modern sermon resulted in the conversion of a Member of Parliament, a distinguished lady and some others, and also in a request for further information, it would not be judged quite a failure! But it is true that we do not hear, in N.T. times, of any Church at Athens. This may be just accidental. Our knowledge of Christian history in the first century is very patchy.

In general, the speech remains a vivid reminder that all preaching of the gospel must find some point of contact with the hearers, and, further, that faith in Christ can hardly be effectively proclaimed apart from faith in One, Living and Eternal, God.

16-17. Paul's response to the blatant idolatry of Athens was vigorous preaching and arguing, in the synagogues, and on the market-place.

18. Epicureans

Followers of Epicurus (341-270 B.C.) The modern use of the word to denote a lover of comfort and pleasure only very partially represents the attitude of the old school of

Epicureans. They had an elaborate philosophy (see esp. Lucretius's *De natura rerum*, conveniently published as a Pelican book), but it is true that their chief aim was ' freedom from care' (Gk. *ataraxia*).

Stoicks

Followers of Zeno 340-268 B.C. Their name is taken from the *Stoa Poikile* (coloured portico), where they taught. The modern use of the word is to describe someone who endures hardship uncomplainingly and again only suggests one aspect of the old Stoic philosophy. Harmony with nature, and obedience to natural law, as the rational element in the Universe, were the main points in the old Stoic school. Seneca and Marcus Aurelius were famous Stoics.

he preached unto them Jesus and the resurrection

This shows that Paul did not ' water down' his message to accommodate it to his critical hearers.

19. Areopagus

Either the Hill of Ares (Mars Hill of A.V.) where the supreme council of Athens had met in early time*s or* the council itself, which now met in Athens. The balance of scholarly opinion favours the latter view.

21. This verse, which describes the Athenian temperament, is suitably written in very stylish Greek.

22. Mars' Hill

See note on v. 19.

23. To the unknown God

Translate ' to an unknown god'. Until recently it was thought that Paul must have adapted an inscription ' to unknown gods', using the singular as it led more easily to his argument for monotheism, but recent opinion is veering

round to think that the singular, *agnōstō theō* would not
have been impossible.

26. of one blood
Omit ' blood ' and read ' of one man ', i.e. Adam.

28. In him we live, and move, and have our being
This is a quotation from Epimenides the Cretan (*c.* 596
B.C.), as we deduce from Clement of Alexandria (*Strom.*
i. 14) and other sources. In Tit. 1.12 another line occurs,
' Cretans are always liars ', and it is from Clement's comment on this verse that we can state the authorship of Paul's
quotation.

As certain also of your own poets have said, For we are also his offspring
This quotation comes from the Cilician poet Aratus
(*Phainomena* 5), where Aratus is following Cleanthes in the
Hymn to Zeus (4).

29. The fact that man can be described as **the offspring
of God** makes it particularly unsuitable to liken God, man's
originator, to something made *by* man, e.g. an idol of gold
or silver.

30. It was part of St. Paul's position that God had not
punished sin in the past as it deserved (cf. Rom. 3.25f.), but
that now a decision had to be made.

31. The specifically Christian part of the address is given
in very condensed form. It stresses (1) the resurrection of
Jesus as proof of God's choice of Him, (2) the future judgment which is committed into His hands.

32-34. Three responses are described: (*a*) mocking, (*b*) desire to hear more, (*c*) conversion. Among those converted
was one member of the Areopagus, Dionysius.

THE CORINTHIAN CHURCH
IS FOUNDED
18.1-17

Owing to the fact that we have in the New Testament two long letters to the Christians of Corinth, we know a good deal about the life of the primitive Church there in the middle of the first century. It is particularly interesting therefore to have in Acts the account of the founding of the Corinthian Church.

Corinth was a big, busy, commercial city, with a reputation for loose living. Paul attaches himself to two Jews from Rome, Aquila and Priscilla, joining with them in their common trade of tent-making. He regularly disputes in the synagogue, according to his usual custom. The arrival of Silas and Timothy brings about some change in his circumstances which causes him to become 'occupied in preaching', his message being that JESUS WAS CHRIST. Once more (v. 6) he turns to the Gentiles. Making the home of Justus (v. 7), a 'God-fearer', his base, he pursues his task, and a leading official of the synagogue is converted. A vision from God (9-10) confirms the outward evidence that he has a big task to do at Corinth, and he stays for eighteen months. As everywhere in Acts, we are made to feel that God takes the initiative.

The trial before Gallio is important partly because it enables us to date these events with more certainty than almost any others in the New Testament. An inscription from Delphi provides evidence that Gallio was pro-consul of Achaia in A.D. 51 (there could be a slight error, but not a big one). Thus we have one fixed point round which many other events can be dated. The story itself shows the pro-consul to be unmoved by Jewish riots. Paul does not have to escape from Corinth, but leaves at his own volition (v. 18).

2. Priscilla and Aquila

We hear of them again in v. 18 and v. 26, also in Rom. 16.3; I Cor. 16.19, and II Tim. 4.19. The decree of expulsion was probably promulgated in A.D. 49-50.

3. he was of the same craft . . . and wrought

Jewish rabbis had to have a secular trade, and Paul apparently carried on with his as a Christian. See also Acts 20.34 and I Thess. 2.9.

5. Paul was pressed in the Spirit

Read 'was occupied in the word'.

8. Crispus

See I Cor. 1.14.

12. Gallio

Junius Gallio, brother of Seneca the philosopher. For his date see above. **Deputy** means pro-consul.

17. All the Greeks

The best texts omit the word *Greeks*, though it is perhaps what was meant. If this Sosthenes is the same as Paul's later companion (see I Cor. 1.1) he must have been converted, like Crispus, another RULER OF THE SYNAGOGUE. If really the *Jews* beat him, perhaps he was already a Christian.

BACK TO ANTIOCH
18.18-22

These few verses describe briefly Paul's return to Antioch, his base, for a short visit. He paid a brief visit to Ephesus, near the west coast of Asia Minor, where later he was to make his longest missionary stay (three years).

18. having shorn his head in Cenchrea: for he had a vow

The 'vow' appears to be a Jewish 'Nazarite' vow, for which see Num. 6.1-21. During this period of a vow (i.e. a period of abstinence of various kinds) the hair was not cut. At the end it was. Two possible explanations are (i) Paul did really observe such Jewish customs for himself, just as he and his fellow teachers were 'fasting' at the time of his original commission from the Antioch Church (Acts 13.1ff.). (ii) Luke puts it in to show that Paul's later action in Acts 21.23ff. is not inconsistent with his general practice, 'unto the Jews I became as a Jew, that I might gain the Jews' (I Cor. 9.20). But one of the difficulties is that, as far as our knowledge goes, a vow had to be ended in the Holy Land.

ON THE WAY TO EPHESUS
18.23

The third missionary journey begins, with a very brief account of the journey through Asia Minor.

23. the country of Galatia and Phrygia

Cf. 16.6. This passage perhaps means 'the Galatian part of Lycaonia, and the whole of Phrygia'. (The whole story of the journey from Corinth to Antioch and back to Ephesus is so brief that it is sometimes thought to be a 'doublet' of the previous trip, Acts 14.26; 15.41; 16.6, etc.)

APOLLOS
18.24-28

This story is difficult to understand fully, but its main point seems to be this. From Alexandria to Ephesus had come one, Apollos, who was a powerful representative of the literary learning of that city.

24. Being a Jew this meant that Apollos was **mighty in the scriptures**, i.e. in the O.T.   He was 'instructed in the way of the Lord', spoke and taught 'the things about Jesus' (this is the correct text, not, with A.V. THE THINGS OF THE LORD), but he knew ONLY THE BAPTISM OF JOHN.   Of the various explanations perhaps the best is that some disciples of Jesus travelled to Alexandria—perhaps Apollos was one of them—knowing our Lord's earlier teaching, but connecting it with the movement of repentance of which John's baptism was the symbol.   Aquila and Priscilla taught him THE WAY OF GOD MORE PERFECTLY, viz. that Jesus was the Messiah.   He then crosses to Achaia (v. 27)—a new start for a man with a new message?—and preaches the gospel. His knowledge of the Old Testament made him a powerful apologist for the Christian faith (21.28).   At Corinth some claimed him as leader of their sect or group ('I of Apollos', I Cor. 1.12), but Paul regarded Apollos' work as complementary to his own (I Cor. 3.).

MORE DISCIPLES OF JOHN WON FOR JESUS CHRIST
19.1-7

Luke clearly means this incident to follow on that of Apollos.   There were twelve men (v. 7) whose position was much the same as that of Apollos.   Is it possible that the word DISCIPLE in v. 1 originally meant 'disciples of Apollos'? Paul, having travelled through 'the higher parts' (A.V., wrongly, THE UPPER COASTS: it means the more northerly of two routes from Pisidian Antioch to Ephesus, the route which passes over the north side of Mt. Messagis, not down the Lycus valley), arrives at Ephesus, and comes in contact with these 'half-believers'.   They had not heard of Christian baptism, carrying with it the gift of the Holy Spirit.   Like Apollos before Priscilla and Aquila took him in hand, they

knew only John's baptism. They were then baptized IN
THE NAME OF THE LORD JESUS (i.e. on confession that 'Jesus
is Lord') and Paul laid his hands on them. This was
followed by evident signs of the coming of the Spirit (v. 6).

There is no absolutely fixed sequence of events in connection with Christian initiation in Acts. The Samaritan converts were baptized by Philip: hands were laid on them by
Peter and John: then the Spirit came. Here the same
apostle baptized (or at least superintends the baptism) and
lays hands: then the Spirit comes. In other cases we do
not read of the laying on of hands (e.g. at Paul's own baptism, by Ananias), and in one case, that of Cornelius, the
Spirit comes first, and then Peter baptizes him. The cases
of the Samaritan converts, and these Ephesians, were those
which were most clearly to foreshadow the usage in the
early Christian centuries.

2. This Ephesian group had not heard that the Holy Spirit
had been given, i.e. that the new age had actually dawned.

PAUL AT EPHESUS
19.8-41

This section describes Paul's long mission at Ephesus, a
town which was to have an important part to play in later
Christian history. One of the main New Testament Epistles
is addressed to the Christians there. One of the brief letters
at the beginning of the Revelation (Rev. 2.1-7) has the same
destination. Ignatius, early in the second century, also
addresses the Church there. Although Paul had paid a
brief visit there (18.19) he may not have been in the strict
sense the founder of the Church. In any case Priscilla and
Aquila had been active during Paul's visit to Antioch.

Paul begins in his usual way by attempting to convince
the Jews in the synagogue (v. 8). Once more opposition

develops, and he SEPARATED THE DISCIPLES (v. 9), i.e. took off those who had accepted the message, and thenceforward taught in the lecture-room of Tyrannus. The Western Text says that he did it 'from the fifth hour to the tenth', i.e. from 11 a.m till 4 p.m. This is probably a shrewd guess, but it suggests that Paul obtained use of the hall during the siesta period, when it would not be in normal use. This continued for two years, and Paul evidently made it a base for an evangelistic movement which spread all around into the province of Asia (v. 10).

One feature of Paul's work was miraculous healing, and just as people had tried to get within reach of Peter's shadow (5.15) they now tried to get contact with Paul by taking handkerchiefs or garments which had been in contact with him to bring healing to those who needed it. To us this seems rather superstitious, but we must remember the story of the woman who was healed by touching Christ's garment. Faith is the real channel of spiritual power, but faith can be expressed in many ways. This led to a kind of pseudo-healing by Jewish exorcists (19.13ff.), who, like Simon Magus, wanted the power of working miracles without understanding what submission to Christ meant. On the occasion referred to in v. 17, the rival healers got the worst of an encounter with a demon-possessed man. This added still more to the prestige of the true preachers and healers, and we read that THE NAME OF THE LORD JESUS WAS MAGNIFIED (v. 17). A special feature of the movement at Ephesus was the voluntary burning of books containing magic secrets, the owners of them now realizing that they were either useless or devilish.

Paul means shortly to go to Macedonia, and sends two colleagues on ahead (21-22). Before he leaves Ephesus, however, a serious anti-Christian riot breaks out. The vested interests of idol makers are threatened by so powerful a movement which seeks to turn men 'from idols, to serve the living and true god' (I Thess. 1.9). A silversmith who makes shrines for Diana (Gk. Artemis, the mother-goddess of Asia) stirs up a big riot, partly led by his fellow craftsmen. The town clerk has to appease the multitude, which he does with great difficulty, telling them to resort to the LAWFUL ASSEMBLY (i.e. the official gathering of the citizens, thrice monthly) if they have a serious case. Once more the official forces of the Roman Empire are shown to be neutral, if not actually benevolent, to the Christian Church.

13. vagabond Jews, exorcists
The word vagabond has changed its meaning since the A.V. was written. 'Itinerant Jewish exorcists.'

14.
A difficult verse, as **Sceva** is not a Jewish name, nor is any such High Priest known. Perhaps the claim to be sons of the High Priest was purely fraudulent.

15.
As in the Gospels, the evil spirit is assumed to belong to the unseen world, and to recognize the presence, or absence, of the power of the Christ.

19. books
i.e. scrolls with magic spells.

21.
This visit to Macedonia was to collect the bounty of the Churches for the poor saints of Jerusalem. The announcement of the plan to visit Rome is important. It is to be fulfilled in the coming chapters, but in an unexpected way. The whole situation is well pictured in Rom. 15.24-27.

29. Gaius and Aristarchus
See note on 20.4.

the theatre
A great place of assembly, now excavated. It held 25,000 people.

31. certain of the chiefs of Asia

Read *certain Asiarchs*. These were important officials, men of dignity rather than of executive authority. Among other things they were responsible for the Imperial cults.

32. assembly

Greek *ecclesia*, the word for the Ephesian assembly of citizens.

33. And they drew Alexander out of the multitude, the Jews putting him forward

An obscure verse, the difficulty arising from the Greek word (*sumbibazō*) translated A.V. 'drew out'. The verse perhaps means 'Some of the crowd supposed that it was to do with Alexander, as the Jews had put him forward'.

35. Town clerk

Greek *grammateus*. The clerk or secretary of the Ephesian *dēmos*, or citizen body.

the city of the Ephesians is a worshipper of the great goddess Diana, and of the image which fell down from Jupiter

Worshipper = temple keeper. The image, etc., is in Greek the one word *Diopetos*, meaning 'that which fell from Zeus', doubtless a treasured meteorite. Many such sacred stones are known to have been venerated in ancient times. Possibly the 'Zeus' in the title was by now little more than a name for 'the sky' (cf. *diipetē hudata*= rain).

37. robbers of churches

Read 'temples'.

38. the law is open and there are deputies

There are assizes and pro-consuls (to preside over them).

PAUL'S BRIEF VISIT TO GREECE
20.1-3

Paul now fulfils the purpose announced in 19.21, and makes his visit to Greece, travelling via Macedonia. V. 3 tells of a plot against him (cf. Rom. 15.23, ' having no more place in these parts '). In view of the plot, he does not sail direct for Syria from Greece, but returns to Asia Minor by the same route as he had come, viz. via Macedonia.

JOURNEY TO TROAS
20.4-5

Representatives of various Churches set out to accompany Paul as he starts for Jerusalem with the bounty collected. These are Sopater (probably Sosipater, of Rom. 16.21), Aristarchus and Secundus, the former having already been with Paul at Ephesus, Gaius (if he is the Macedonian Gaius mentioned in 19.29, *Derbe* should read *Doberius* as given in the Western text, for Doberius is in Macedonia), Timothy, Tychicus and Trophimus. The latter two appear respectively in Col. 4.7f. and Acts 21.29, also in the Pastoral Epistles. This party precedes Paul, and awaits him at Troas. This large deputation shows what importance Paul attached to this collection, probably seeing in it an important contribution to the coherence of the Jewish and Gentile Churches. As a ' we passage ' begins at v. 5, we assume Luke accompanies Paul from Philippi.

A WEEK AT TROAS
20.6-12

After Passover (' unleavened bread ' followed immediately

on the great festival) Paul's party crossed to Troas, and
waited there a week, which culminated in a Sunday gathering of the Church. This passage is extremely important,
for it gives us our earliest *narrative* account of a Sunday
meeting. There are plain suggestions elsewhere that the
Christians met on the first day of the week (e.g. the two
appearances of the Risen Lord in John 20, the command
to put by for the collection 'on the first day of the week',
I Cor. 16.2, the vision given to John the Seer 'on the Lord's
Day', Rev. 1.10), but here we have a definite statement that
they did so gather, and TO BREAK BREAD. Although this
phase can have a purely practical meaning (i.e. to take food),
it certainly here means the Eucharist (cf. I Cor. 10.16-17;
I Cor. 11.20-34). Similarity to later custom puts this
practically beyond doubt. Paul's long discourse, accompanied by the heavy atmosphere, produced by the 'many
lights' causes Eutychus to fall from the third-story window.
(The house must have been of fair size. It was many years
—about 250—before the Christians had any churches of
their own, so big houses were in demand for worship.) A
miracle, or apparent miracle, restores him, and the ceremony
is resumed.

11. when he . . . had broken bread and eaten

There may be here a reference to the formal breaking of
bread, and to the ordinary meal which followed it, sometimes known as the *agape* (cf. Pliny's letter to Trajan, *Epp.*
10, and *Correspondence of Trajan, Epp.* 96). The Synoptic
Gospels tell the story of the Last Supper including the words
'This is my body' etc., though only Luke—and not all texts
of Luke—follows Paul in giving an actual command to continue the rite. The universal custom of doing so in the early
Church is the best support for the fundamental historicity of
the Gospel tradition.

TROAS TO MILETUS
20.13-16

These verses describe the sea-journey down the coast to
Miletus, the port for Ephesus. Notice the clear separation
of the author's party from Paul in 13-14. The places can
be seen on the map.

PAUL'S PASTORAL CHARGE
20.17-38

As Paul has not time to get the thirty miles from Miletus
to Ephesus, he sends for THE ELDERS OF THE CHURCH, so
that he may give them a final charge. Later (v. 28) the
audience are described as BISHOPS (*episkopoi*), and this is
perhaps the clearest evidence in the New Testament that at
this stage 'bishops' and 'presbyters' were the same. Both
functions were similar to that of the Jewish 'elders'. The
speech can be divided up as follows. (1) 18-21 Reminder
of Paul's pastoral record. (2) 22-27 Announcement of Paul's
expected suffering. (3) 28-31 Exhortation to faithfulness
in pastoral work. (4) 32-35 Commendation. The divisions
are not exact, and (1)—Paul's own record—comes in almost
as a kind of refrain, in vv. 26-27, 31, 33, etc.

The spirit of the whole speech is very much like that of
the Pastoral Epistles, where, as here, Paul is represented as
giving a final charge to ministers of the Church (Timothy
and Titus stand in a special category, between that of apostle
and presbyter). Like the Pastoral Epistles, this passage
may be intended to convey to readers the conviction that
the institution of the pastoral ministry had apostolic authority behind it.

18-21. For Paul's reference to his own previous service, cf.
I Thess. 1.5; 2.2, etc.

21. Repentance toward God, and faith toward our Lord Jesus Christ

This summary of the Christian message fits in with Paul's description of his mission in I Thess. 1.9, and also with other chapters in Acts, e.g. Acts 17, Paul's speech at Athens.

22. Paul's announcement of coming suffering corresponds to our Lord's frequent warnings of His coming Passion.

23. The Holy Ghost witnesses **in every city,** i.e. through the mouths of prophets in each congregation.

24. Paul always relates the gospel to God, never resting in a purely Christ-centred faith, e.g. Phil. 2.11.

25. One of the few places in Acts where Paul is said to preach **the kingdom of God.** (See also 19.8; 28.31.)

28. The Church is called **a flock.** Cf. Luke 12.32; I Peter 5.2; John 21.15-17.

It is the Holy Ghost who has appointed the elders as 'overseers' or bishops (from *episkopoi*), presumably by the testimony of prophets, and by the gift given in the laying on of hands. (See I Tim. 4.14; II Tim. 1.6).

the church of God, which he hath purchased with his own blood.

The Greek should be translated: which he purchased with the blood of His Own, i.e. His Own Son. Notice that Acts, which is sometimes said to have only a 'weak' doctrine of the atonement, treats the Cross as the means whereby the Church has been **purchased** for God. Cf. I Peter 1.18-19.

30-31. The prophecy of coming heretical teachers is in line with warnings reported to be given by Christ in His 'apocalyptic' teaching. See, e.g., Mark 13.22-23.

32. I commend you to God, and to the word of his grace

Paul treats 'the Gospel' as a living force, by means of which God's care of the Ephesians will be made a reality. The **inheritance among them that are sanctified** is reminiscent again of I Peter 1.4.

34. For Paul's self-supporting work, cf. 18.3, and note *ad loc.*

35. It is more blessed to give than to receive

A very important verse: the only actual words of Jesus recorded in the New Testament outside the Gospels. The saying is referred to in I Clement 2.1. It is possibly in both cases a summary of Christ's teaching in Luke 6.38.

36-38. The sad farewell is meant to lead up to the 'Passion Narrative' of the coming chapters. It is clear that Luke is unaware of any further visit of Paul to Ephesus, and hence it is difficult to fit in a further visit, such as is contemplated in I and II Timothy.

IX

PAUL'S PASSION NARRATIVE
21–27

JOURNEY TO JERUSALEM
21.1-16

Like his Master, Paul now has to go up to Jerusalem. The journey itself is uneventful—its course can easily be traced on the map. The first point of interest is the warning given to Paul at Tyre (v. 4) THROUGH THE SPIRIT that he should not go up to Jerusalem. This does not mean, we must presume, that his visit was really contrary to the mind of the Spirit. Luke is building up the sense that terrible things await Paul there. At Caesarea, Philip the Evangelist appears again. He was last heard of in 8.40, when he arrived at Caesarea from Azotus. As Paul now stayed with him MANY DAYS, he may well have derived much of the material in the early chapters, particularly that relating to the Caesarean mission, from him and his family. We notice in passing that Philip has four virgin daughters, who prophesied, i.e. spoke under the Spirit's influence. Perhaps it was daughters of this type that Paul has in mind in I Cor. 7.34-36. Another link with the earlier chapters occurs in v. 10, where Agabus, whom we remember as the prophet who foretold the famine (11.28), arrives on the scene again, and, by the acted parable of the girdle, warns Paul not to go to the capital. When he says that Paul will be delivered INTO THE HANDS OF THE GENTILES we cannot help being reminded of our Lord's prophecy of His own fate (Mark

10.38). Paul is affected by the urgent appeals of his friends, but protests his willingness for suffering and sacrifice. THE WILL OF THE LORD BE DONE reply his friends, echoing Christ's words in Gethsemane.

15. we took up our carriages
Possibly ' prepared horses', or just ' made preparations '.

16. Translate with R.V.: ' And there went with us also certain of the disciples from Caesarea, bringing with them one Mnason of Cyprus, an early disciple, with whom we should lodge.' Probably Mnason lived, or had friends, near Jerusalem. In the city itself, Paul probably had sufficient links, but he may have preferred to stay outside the city, just as Jesus stayed at Bethany.

PAUL'S RECEPTION AT JERUSALEM
21.17-26

This is an important section of the narrative, but not without its difficulties. In the first place it shows clearly that by this time James was the undisputed head of the Jerusalem Church, though he was supported by a group of elders. Also it is clear that James was particularly sensitive about the feelings of the Jewish Christians, and anxious for them not to be offended by Paul's more liberal approach. In v. 20 he says that there are MANY THOUSANDS of Jews who believe, and they are all ZEALOUS FOR THE LAW. 'Jews' means, probably, 'men of Judaea'—'many thousands' would be a large number for Jerusalem itself. They must have come mainly from the Pharisaic party, as they seem to have been upset by rumours that Paul was teaching *Jews* (not only Gentiles) that circumcision was unnecessary (v. 21).

James proposes a curious line of action. He says that

there are four men who have taken a vow—presumably a
Nazarite one (cf. 18.18). If during the period of the vow
the one who had made it incurred defilement, he had to
shave his head, make certain offerings and start all over
again. (See Num. 6.2ff.) A similar process was necessary
at the end of the consecrated period. Apparently these four
men wanted to go through this process, and James asks Paul
to pay for their offerings, as a sign that he was a devout
follower of the Law. What is curious is that Paul is told
to purify himself with them. There is some evidence that
generous benefactors sometimes paid the costs of 'purification' offerings, and that in these cases the benefactors
were expected themselves to undergo purificatory rites.
Clearly Paul could hardly appear in a more law-abiding role
than that of the generous supporter of devout men anxious
to fulfil the law's requirements. Perhaps one point in
Luke's mind is to show how extremely unreasonable was the
Jewish attitude. Paul was attacked and arrested at the very
time when he was being most punctilious for the Law.
It certainly seems strange to find the fiery anti-legalist of
Galatians accepting the role here described, but it is not
impossible that he found expediency wise at times.

19-20. Luke presents a picture of the leaders of the Jerusalem Church warmly accepting the news of Paul's Gentile
mission. Perhaps, as often, the leaders were more advanced
than the rank and file.

25. It is odd that James tells Paul about the apostolic decree, for Paul himself had been one of the chief bearers of
it (16.4).

26. entered into the temple
  The verb is imperfect and perhaps means 'used to enter
the Temple', i.e. until all the offerings for each man was
complete.

THE TEMPLE RIOT
21.27-40

When the period of purification (seven days) was almost
up, Jews from Asia, who knew of Paul's belief and practice,
saw him in the Temple, and made a vigorous complaint
against him. Having seen him with Trophimus the Ephesian
(cf. 20.4) in the city they accuse him of bringing him into
the Temple. Perhaps they mistook one of the Nazarite
devotees for Trophimus. Luke means us to notice how
wild and fanatical was the Jewish opposition to Paul. Paul
narrowly escapes a lynching, but is dramatically rescued by
the CHIEF CAPTAIN (military tribune of the cohort, a Roman
officer, of approximately the same rank as a Lieutenant-
Colonel in the British Army). The tribune and his men are
carrying Paul into THE CASTLE, i.e. tower of Antonia, with
the people shouting AWAY WITH HIM, just as they had done
twenty-five years earlier during the trial of Jesus, when
Paul gains permission to address the people. He gets this
permission after surprising the tribune by addressing him
in Greek, the language of polite intercourse and of com-
merce in the Roman Empire. The tribune had mistaken
him for a well-known Egyptian revolutionary (see below).
Paul makes his famous claim (v. 39) to be A CITIZEN OF NO
MEAN CITY—Tarsus—and is given leave to address the
crowd from the steps, which he does, speaking now in
Aramaic, which is what v. 40 means by HEBREW.

29. It was punishable by death for a Gentile to pass beyond
the barrier which separated the Court of the Gentiles
from the Holy Place. St. Paul refers to this barrier as ' the
middle wall of partition ', broken down by Christ (Eph.
2.14).

For **Trophimus**, see 20.4.

34. the certainty

Almost the same word (*asphales* for *asphaleia*) as is used in Luke 1.4. Luke wrote so that Theophilus might know 'the certainty' about Christianity. Like this tribune, he perhaps found it difficult to discern, among the fanatical complaints of the Jews.

38. that Egyptian

Only a few years previously, an Egyptian had led a big force against Jerusalem (Josephus says 30,000; Luke is more moderate—he says 4,000), and though repelled by Felix, escaped himself. The tribunal fears that he has returned. (See Josephus, *Jewish War*, 2, 134f., *Antiquities*, 20.8.6.) The Egyptian followers are called murderers, literally *Sicarii*, dagger-men.

PAUL'S EXPLANATION AND ITS REJECTION BY THE CROWD
22.1-23

Paul now recounts his conversion story, the narrative keeping fairly closely to that already given in Acts 9.1-18, except for some insignificant variations. He stresses to this audience his previous strict loyalty to the Law (see 3-5). One or two interesting biographical points come out, for which see the notes below. At the end of the story of the conversion he recounts an experience of which we do not hear elsewhere, viz. how he had a vision in the Temple at Jerusalem (v. 17), in which he was told that he must leave Jerusalem, and address his mission to the Gentiles.

In the notes below, comment is made only on fresh points in the conversion story.

3. brought up in this city at the feet of Gamaliel

Presumably the same Gamaliel as we met in 5.34. There

Gamaliel is shown as a tolerant and liberal-minded Rabbi,
and he may have contributed to Paul's conversion, by his
open-minded attitude, although the young pupil was for a
time 'exceedingly mad' against the Christians.

9. they heard not the voice
Cf. Acts 9.7, THE MEN WHICH JOURNEYED WITH HIM STOOD
SPEECHLESS, HEARING A VOICE, BUT SEEING NO MAN. Those
who are troubled by this apparent contradiction avoid it by
distinguishing between 'the voice' which they did not hear
and 'the sound' which they did (R.V. marg.). Meticulous
agreement in tiny details is not a necessary sign of true
tradition; it may denote just the opposite.

12. It is stressed here that Ananias stood well with the local
Jews. He must however have been a Christian, as he tells
Paul to ARISE, AND BE BAPTIZED (v. 16).

14. that Just One
A description of Jesus, cf. 3.14.

17. This vision is best placed before Paul's departure for
Tarsus, recorded in 9.30. It is interesting to see that even
after his conversion, Paul still prayed in the Temple, as Peter
and John had done.

20. Paul repeats his share in responsibility for Stephen's
death. Notice that Stephen is called here a **martyr,** which
in Greek is *martus*, witness. But already the word was
beginning to mean 'witness by death'.

23. Signs of passionate horror and disgust.

THE ROMANS ONCE MORE REGRET
MALTREATING PAUL
22.24-30

Now the tribune decides that he must take Paul into safe
custody, but like Pilate, he makes the mistake of deciding
to scourge his prisoner, although not convinced of his guilt.
Paul protests (v. 25), for Romans were not subject to such
treatment. This leads to the famous dialogue between Paul
and the tribune, who says that he purchased his citizenship,
while Paul is able to claim citizenship from birth (v. 28).
Regretting his rash action, the tribune takes refuge in calling
the Sanhedrin (cf. John 18.31, ' Take ye him, and judge him
according to your law '). The apostle shares almost all the
indignities of the Master.

25. bound him with thongs
  ' Stretched him for the lashes.'

28. Citizenship could be bought, particularly in the reign
of Claudius (A.D. 41-54). It had evidently been conferred
on some ancestor of Paul, we know not for what reason.
The ' Western text ' reads, ' I know with how great a sum I
obtained this citizenship ', and this can be taken ironically—
' I know how cheap citizenship is nowadays '. Some commentators are attracted by this reading, but the usual text
fits much more easily into the context.

FAILURE OF THE COUNCIL TO
SETTLE PAUL'S CASE
23.1-11

Paul, like his Master, now appears before the Sanhedrin,
but like Him, at a special rather than a regular meeting.

The important thing to notice is that this attempt of the tribune to shift the responsibility on to the Jews fails. Once more (v. 10) the tribune has to take Paul back to the castle. This is the *motif* of all these next chapters. Each authority tries to escape the responsibility of decision: Claudius Lysias puts the case before the Jews, then has to refer it to the governor, Felix. Felix temporized for two years, so the case came to Festus, his successor. Festus tries once more to put it to the Jews, with the result that Paul (25.11) appeals to Caesar. This brings Paul eventually to Rome. Surely Luke is saying to Theophilus: 'You cannot escape the challenge of Christ by putting it all down to a sectarian clash among the Jews. The Roman Empire must face the challenge, and come to grips with the great message of the gospel.'

The incidents in the Sanhedrin are more important as throwing light on Jewish custom and beliefs than for their intrinsic importance in the story of Acts. Paul begins by claiming to have lived strictly according to Jewish law, and is rudely interrupted by the High Priest. Paul replies vigorously, and like his Master, is asked whether he dares so to speak to the High Priest (cf. John 18.22). He claims ignorance of the fact that his accuser *was* High Priest, but rapidly moves on to another line of defence. He knows that the Sanhedrin is made up of Sadducees, the worldly, old-fashioned, politically minded party, and the more devout party of the Pharisees, who had accepted the newer beliefs in the resurrection after death, angels, spirits, etc. Paul, who had been a Pharisee (Phil. 3.5) claims still to stand with them against the Sadducees. There was truth in this, for Christians certainly believed in resurrection. The claim however produces a split, and once more (v. 10) Paul has to be taken into the castle. The Romans have not escaped from their dilemma yet! On the contrary, Paul has taken his first step to Rome, and in a vision (v. 11) God assures him that he will yet witness for Him there.

2. Ananias
High Priest, A.D. 47-58/9.

3. Whited wall
Nobody quite knows why this was a term of rebuke, but 'whitened tomb' is used in a derogatory sense in Matt. 23.27.

5. Thou shalt not speak evil, etc.
Ex. 22.28.

6ff. Pharisees and Sadducees. The description of the respective beliefs of the two sects fits in with what we read in other parts of the N.T. and in Josephus.

9. a spirit or an angel
The Pharisees interpret Paul's conversion experience in accordance with their own special beliefs.

11. This vision balances that described in 22.17-21. It also provides an example of Paul receiving God's grace in a time of special trouble and difficulty (cf. II Cor. 12.9).

A PLOT FAILS
23.12-22

The story of the plot against Paul emphasizes the fanatical hatred of the Jews against him, and indirectly compels the tribune to send him to greater safety at Caesarea, the official headquarters of the province.

16. It would seem that Paul's sister and her son lived at Jerusalem, but this may not have been so. They may have been there for the feast of Pentecost.

PAUL IS SENT TO CAESAREA
23.23-35

The tribune now dispatches Paul to Caesarea, with a really strong guard, four hundred soldiers on foot, and seventy cavalry. He also writes a letter (25-30) explaining the position.

24. Felix the governor
Felix became procurator of Judaea in A.D. 52. He held the same post as Pontius Pilate (A.D. 26-36), but there had been various other arrangements in the interval.

26-30. The letter gives a very fair and concise account of the problem, though it is not exact in every detail.

31. Antipatris
About two-thirds of the distance to Caesarea.

34-35. The passage is difficult. It seems to suggest that Felix would have liked to get out of the responsibility, but as Paul was of the Province of Cilicia he might have done so, for Cilicia came under the governor of Syria. Probably the real interest is theological. Pilate had asked where Jesus came from (Luke 23.6), and finding that He came from Galilee sent Him to Herod. Felix, finding Paul is a Cilician, gives orders for him to be kept in *Herod's* praetorium, i.e. palace.

PAUL BEFORE FELIX
24

We now come to the first of three chapters which may strike the reader as rather repetitive, and perhaps a little wearisome. They contain 'hearings' of Paul's case—perhaps 'trials' is too formal a word—before Felix, before Festus, his successor as governor, and before Agrippa, a neighbouring puppet king. The case against him, stated or implied, is that of the fanatical and hostile Jews. On the whole, the Roman authorities are shown to be unconvinced by the Jews, and either partial to Paul, or at least inclined to treat him with fairness and tolerance, while unwilling either to face the odium which a clear-cut acquittal would bring with it, or to accept the moral and spiritual results of believing his message. This part of the book has three main purposes. (1) It shows how God's purpose of bringing Paul to Rome was providentially brought about, almost in spite of human plans and purposes. (2) It gives a final opportunity for Paul to make an extended apologia for his faith, particularly in relation to the Old Testament revelation. (3) It is of particular interest to readers like Theophilus, who, as Roman officials have to make up their minds what attitude they are to take up to the new religion.

In this chapter vv. 1-9 describe the speech against Paul made by Tertullus, a professional lawyer, and in vv. 10-21, Paul replies. Vv. 22-27 give Felix's reaction, ending with his keeping Paul as a prisoner for two years, not because of proved guilt, but as a step which he thought expedient as a means of keeping in good odour with the Jews.

1. The importance of the case in the eyes of the Jews is shown by the fact that the High Priest himself visits Caesarea to pursue it.

2-4. The usual complimentary opening of such a speech.

5. sect of the Nazarenes

The Greek word translated sect is *hairesis* (English, heresy), which at this time meant a section or group. In Acts (see especially 24.14) it already seems to have a slightly

critical flavour. *Nazarene:* only here and in Matt. 2.23.
The primary meaning seems to be 'inhabitant of Nazareth'
or a follower of such an inhabitant, but there are real etymo-
logical difficulties, and perhaps some reference to the Old
Testament 'Nazirites' (see B.C., Vol. V, Add. Note, 30).

11. twelve days

Luke adds together the seven days of 21.27 and the five
days 24.1. This leaves no time for the journey to Caesarea,
and some have felt compelled to interpret 21.27 as marking
the beginning of the 'seven days' purification, rather than
the end. But, as 21.27 says the seven days 'were going to
be' fulfilled, there might still be a day or two left for the
journey.

14. Paul stresses the real continuity between his Christian
faith and the message of the Old Testament (as he does in
his epistles, e.g. in Rom. 9–11 and 15.4).

17. Paul regards his offering 'for the poor saints at Jerusalem' as made to his nation. Is it possible that the gift was
not intended to be confined to Christian Jews?

21. Paul goes back to his statement about the resurrection,
which divided the Pharisees from the Sadducees (23.6).

22. having more perfect knowledge

Luke uses the same word *akribōs*—here used in the com-
parative form—as he used in Luke 1.3, to describe the
accurate way in which he had investigated everything about
Christianity. Throughout these trial scenes, he clearly has
Theophilus very much in mind.

23. The balance of Felix's judgment is favourable to Paul

24. Drusilla, younger daughter of Herod Agrippa I.

25-26. Felix's attitude, like that of Pontius Pilate, was one
of dangerous compromise. He was clearly challenged and
stirred by the message, but love of money and popularity
were allowed to cloud his sense of justice and the dictates
of his conscience.

27. after two years

There has been much ink spilt over the date of the arrival
of Festus. Certain statements of Tacitus would appear to
make the change of governor take place before A.D. 55, but
according to the chronology of Acts, it ought to be about
A.D. 57 or 58.

PAUL BEFORE FESTUS
25.1-12

Now the story is repeated, after the arrival of the new
governor. The High Priest and his party resume their
efforts to get Paul condemned, especially desiring him to
be brought to Jerusalem (v. 3) where if necessary an un-
official lynching might take place. Festus checks this desire,
and promises to resume the examination at Caesarea. In
v. 9 he asks Paul if he will go to Jerusalem, and at this point
Paul decides to appeal to Caesar himself. The right of
appeal to Caesar was a valuable right belonging only to
Roman citizens. It was to have far-reaching results in
Paul's case.

PAUL AND AGRIPPA
25.13–26.32

Just as Jesus and Peter had both been brought before
courts of the Herodian dynasty, Paul in his turn has to stand
a 'trial' before a Herod, this time Herod Agrippa II, son

of Agrippa I, of whom we read in chapter 12. He was by this time king of the area based on Caesarea Philippi (to be distinguished from the Caesarea where the present story is taking place). Bernice was his *sister*, not his wife, though the possibility of an incestuous union is not to be ruled out. In 13-21 of chapter 25 we see Festus giving an account of Paul's case to Agrippa, who has doubtless come on a courtesy visit to the new governor. His description is a typical colonial servant's account of a case in which he has a fairly accurate, though not an inside knowledge of a local religious dispute. In 25.22 Agrippa expresses a desire to see Paul (cf. Luke 23.8, where Herod Antipas had been desirous to see Jesus for a long season). 25.23–26.32 describes the ever-memorable scene of Paul's appearance before Agrippa.

25.26. no certain things
Luke wrote that Theophilus might know 'the certainty' (the same Greek word as here)—another link between these chapters and the opening of Luke's Gospel.

26.4-7. Paul still takes his stand on his fundamental loyalty to what he feels is the real Judaism. For v. 5, cf. Phil. 3.4-6.

10. I gave my voice against them
The words rather suggest that Paul was a member of the Sanhedrin. The word translated 'voice' should be translated 'vote', but even this might be used in a semi-metaphorical sense.

12-18. This is the third account of the conversion, and is specially notable for 16-18, where the commission to preach to the Gentiles is given at the moment of the vision itself. V. 18 is particularly important as a primitive description of the apostolic mission. It is very close to St. Paul's description of his work in Thessalonica (see I Thess. 1.9-10). The

main features of the message to Gentiles were: turn to God from idols, receive forgiveness, look for your share in the coming victory of Christ.

22-23. Paul follows the same line as is recorded in Luke 24 of our Lord, showing that the death of the Christ was really in harmony with the teaching of the Old Testament. The mention of light for the Gentiles is not made there, but is mentioned in the Infancy narrative in Luke (see especially Luke 2.32).

24-28. The first reaction of Festus is one of supercilious contempt, but does Agrippa so receive Paul's personal challenge in v. 27, where an appeal is made to Agrippa's supposed loyalty to Judaism? V. 28, **Almost thou persuadest me to be a Christian**, is now usually taken to be spoken ironically. The exact translation of the words is by no means easy. It could be ' In short, you are persuading me to play the Christian ' (with or without a question mark). But it could be ' with a little effort you are persuading me (or ' do you persuade me ') to play the Christian '. There is a play on words in Paul's reply, ' I would to God, that not only thou, but also all that hear me this day, were—*with little or much* (*effort*) —such as I am.'

We cannot forbear to quote a paragraph from Dean Vaughan's *Church of the First Days* (Macmillan, 1890, first published 1864), a collection of sermon-lectures on the Acts unsurpassed in accurate scholarship and expository power.

' King Agrippa, like Felix and Festus, like his ancestors in the sacred story, flits now from the scene. Nothing came, we believe, of this strange interview between light and darkness, between sin and the gospel. Agrippa kept his useless, idle faith in the Jewish scriptures, kept too his heart's lust, his obscene idol, his earth-bounded life. Times of trial drew on: in the last Jewish wars he sided with the Romans;

and then retired to drag out an inglorious age through
thirty uneventful years, with a titular royalty and in real
servitude, under the imperial shadow at Rome. In the year
of our Lord 100, being the third year of the Emperor
Trajan, he died there; the last prince of the bloodstained race
of Herod. Yet, like all whose names, for good or ill, are
once stamped upon the holy page, Agrippa remains to all
time for the edification and instruction of the Church which
he despised.'[1]

31-32. At Paul's third large-scale hearing, he is once more
declared innocent of any capital offence. Luke makes it
clear that the journey to Rome, now about to commence,
is the result of Paul's insistence on his rights, not of any
clear agreement as to his guilt.

THE VOYAGE AND SHIPWRECK
27

This long chapter records the exciting journey of Paul
and his companions from Caesarea until the shipwreck on
Malta. Its significance in Acts should be clearly understood. (1) It is a well-told story and as such makes its
contribution to the literary balance of the book. Luke was
far from ignoring this aspect of the matter, though we need
not assume that the story has no good historical basis. The
first person is used repeatedly in the chapter. (2) The shipwreck, to which all is heading, represents both the lowest
ebb of Paul's fortunes, and his unexpected hope, suddenly
revived, of reaching Rome after all. Thus it is not fanciful
to regard it as in some way symmetrical with the Cross itself in Luke's Gospel. (3) It is particularly designed to
bring out how superior was Paul's knowledge, advice and
courage to that of the centurion and the crew. We are

[1] op. cit., p. 574.

meant to feel that God was on Paul's side, supporting and
guiding him. Jonah all but brought disaster to *his* ship,
for he was flying against the clear guidance of God (Jonah
1.11-12). Paul's ship, on the contrary, would certainly have
foundered, and its crew and passengers have been lost, had
not God intended to bring Paul safe to Rome. Only when
these points have been grasped is it worthwhile to study the
geographical and nautical aspects of the narrative. Many
commentaries get so involved in these details that the theological importance of the narrative is all but ignored. (On
the nautical aspects of the chapter, see James Smith, *The
Voyage and Shipwreck of St. Paul*, London, 1848—still
interesting.)

1. Augustus's band

It is not known how this 'band' was connected with the
Emperor. Perhaps it had an honourable title, something
like the 'King's Royal Rifles'.

2. Adramyttium

A town in Mysia, now Asia Minor.

Aristarchus

The same man as we heard of in 19.29 and 20.4.

3. The centurion is living up to the general reputation of
Roman officials in Acts—that of being tolerant and friendly
to Christians.

4. sailed under Cyprus

i.e. under its shelter, in this case east of it.

5. The ship made its way along the south coast of Asia
Minor till it reached *Myra* (for which see map).

6. There was a regular service of wheat boats from
Alexandria to Italy.

7. Not being able to make headway against the N.W. wind the ship made its way S.W., passing by the eastern end of Crete (Cape Salmone).

8. There is a bay named in modern times Limeonas Kalous (cf. Greek of Acts *Kalous Limenas*), just east of Cape Matala, midway along the south coast of Crete, but its identification with Luke's **fair havens** is not absolutely certain.

9. The fast
   i.e. the day of Atonement, which fell in A.D. 59 on October 5th. Sailing was dangerous so late in the season.

10. Paul, acting as a prophet, foretells—though not with absolute accuracy—the ill results of leaving harbour.

12. Apparently a short voyage along to Phenice was all that was intended.

an haven of Crete, and lieth toward the south-west and north-west
   The Greek itself is not easy to translate, and A.V. is probably not far wrong. R.V. is almost certainly erroneous. It reads ' looking north-east and south-east '. R.V. margin ('looking down the south-west wind and down the north-west wind ') explains how the translators arrived at their extraordinary translation. They translate *kata liba kai kata chorōn* as looking *along the line* of the S.W. and N.W. winds, i.e. N.E. and S.E. This error arose from thinking that the harbour had been rightly identified as *Lutro*, which does face the sea with its coasts at such an angle. Modern scholars usually identify Phenice with *Phenike*, which faces the way Luke describes. (For an excellent note, see Page, *Acts of the Apostles*, Macmillan, 1900, pp. 254-256.)

14. The good hopes raised in v. 13 did not last long. A
'typhonic' wind rushed down from the Cretan mountains.

Euroclydon

In A.V. is a corruption of *Euraquilo,* a wind with
northerly and easterly elements, actually E.N.E. Phenike
(see above) would have provided protection from just such
a wind.

16. Being driven before the wind (see v. 15) they ran under
the temporary shelter of Cauda (now Gozzo) S.W. of Crete.
Here they managed to haul in the dinghy.

17. They took measures to strengthen the ship (probably
with ropes or planks). If ropes were used, **undergirding
the ship** *may* mean passing ropes right round the hull,
but it is quite uncertain how the 'helps' were actually
used. They still feared that they would be driven right
across the Mediterranean into **the quicksands**, i.e. Syrtis,
west of Cyrene, so 'lowered the gear' to reduce wind-
pressure.

21-26. These verses record Paul's reassuring speech to the
crew. His confidence is based on a vision in which God
assures him that he **must be brought before Caesar**. Paul
plays exactly the opposite part to that played by Jonah.

27. Adria

Not the modern Adriatic, but the whole mid-Mediter-
ranean area. As they are soon to arrive at Malta (see 28.1)
we must think that the wind had veered round to the east,
or else that by skilful manœuvre they had managed to keep
their course more or less W.N.W. Noise of waves breaking
on rocks would suggest the presence of land.

29. Anyone who knows the rocky coast of Malta will realize that this was no idle fear. They took the unusual step of casting their anchors out of the stern, so as to keep the ship pointing to the land.

30-32. The sailors were going to escape by the boat, but this step is prevented by Paul's foresight. The sailors are going to be needed again in 40-41.

33-38. There is more in this story of Paul encouraging the crew and passengers to take food than might appear on the surface. It cannot mean that for fourteen days they had actually taken *nothing*—they would have starved. Probably the meaning is that in their fear and anxiety they are partially fasting, hoping thereby to placate their heathen gods and make them propitious. Perhaps sea-sickness had played its part. In contrast, Paul has perfect trust in God, and gives **thanks to God in presence of them all**, after which they eat and are strengthened. It is said that any thought of the Eucharist is absurd in such a context. But we must note: (1) The actual word *eucharistēsen*, he gave thanks, is used (v. 35). (2) Paul, being full of praise and thanks for the now hoped-for deliverance, may well have had in his mind that greater deliverance for which he regularly ' gave thanks ' at the solemn meal of the Eucharist. This is not to say that he included any reference to the Passion of Christ in his thanksgiving. If Luke thinks of the moment of shipwreck as in some way balancing the actual death of Jesus, another parallel will suggest itself— does this meal correspond to the Last Supper? (3) Is there yet another meaning? If Theophilus had any ideas about the Eucharist being a secret and unhealthy rite, did Luke mean to stress ' he gave thanks to God *before them all* '? (Cf. Pliny's Letter to Trajan, ' Their custom was to depart and meet together again to take food, but ordinary and harmless food.' *Epp.* 10.96.)

37. two hundred three score and sixteen souls

The better texts read seventy-six, but it is possible the larger number is correct. It would not be as large as other known complements of ancient ships.

38. Means that, with land so near, it was possible to lighten the ship still further.

39-41. These verses record the actual wreck. The traditional site is St. Paul's Bay, Malta, and very careful examination by modern scholars has confirmed this tradition. James Smith, in the work already quoted, examined every detail of the topography, and even the most radical scholars tend to accept the identification. In the northern part of Malta on the east coast is a bay with inlets leading in to the west. Almost joining the northern extremity of the bay are two little islands, on the larger of which is a striking monument to St. Paul. The view of Smith is that one of the inlets is the **creek** of v. 39, and that the channel between the larger island and the mainland is **the place where two seas met** of v. 41. It should be mentioned that there is no longer **a shore** to the creek, but that may have been washed away. Also the Greek word translated **where two seas met** is *dithalatton* which *may* mean a reef or shoal. The whole aspect of the coast is barren and rock-bound, and a safe landing on it under conditions like those described would certainly be regarded as a miracle.

40. Read: *having cast off the anchors they left them in the sea* (not as in A.V.); for **loosed the rudder bands** read: *unleashed the paddle-rudders*; for **mainsail** read *foresail*. (Greek, *artemōn.*) The running aground in v. 41 is clearly not what was hoped for, and is in some way connected with THE PLACE WHERE TWO SEAS MET.

42-44. Here we have the last hazards overcome: (*a*) The soldiers, but for the centurion, would have killed the prisoners. This was overcome by the centurion's order. (b) The final trip from the wreck to the shore had to be made by swimming or on planks and broken pieces of ship. All survived both, thus fulfilling Paul's prophecy in v. 24. The theme of the book, 'Nothing can stop the gospel', has had one more striking illustration.

XII

VICTORY
28

We now come to the triumphant conclusion of the book. All perils past, Paul stays for a few days in Malta, and the power of Christ is made manifest there as elsewhere. Paul is debtor both to the Greeks and the barbarians, and is ready to act in faith wherever the providence of God brings him. From there he makes his way to Rome, where he is allowed to give his message to the Jews. Their reception of him is half-hearted and suspicious, and Paul rebukes them in the same words as his Master had used of their fellow-countrymen in Palestine. He announces that the gospel is now for the Gentiles and that they will hear. The last verses of the book describe him PREACHING THE KING-DOM OF GOD, AND TEACHING THOSE THINGS WHICH CONCERN THE LORD JESUS CHRIST WITH ALL CONFIDENCE, NO MAN FORBIDDING HIM.

PAUL AT MALTA
28.1-10

After the miraculous escape, the party realize that the island on which they have landed is Malta. The people witness a surprising incident in which Paul calmly shakes off a viper which has clung to his hand, and after thinking he is a murderer (v. 4) go to the other extreme and think he is a god (v. 6). The Roman official in charge of the island receives them courteously for three days, and Paul is able

to heal his father, who has dysentery (v. 8). These verses
have a strong medical colouring. The whole stay lasts for
three months.

4. vengeance

In Greek, *dikē*, probably meaning a goddess whose task
it was to see that justice was done.

7. chief man

There is inscriptional evidence for the title 'chief' as the
description of the governor of Malta. (See *Beginnings*, Vol.
iv, p. 342.)

EASY JOURNEY TO ROME
28.11-16

As if to suggest that difficulties were temporarily at an
end, the remaining journey goes unexpectedly smoothly. In
a ship with the name or sign Castor and Pollux (patrons of
navigation) the party goes on to Syracuse, a journey which
now takes one night, and may then have taken somewhat
longer, but perhaps not much longer in good conditions.
From there they go to Rhegium (modern Reggio) on the
west coast of the toe of Italy in the straits of Messina. In
one good day's run they come to Puteoli, near the present
city of Naples. Somehow the party contrives to stay for
seven days there with the Christians (Puteoli was an important commercial harbour, and Christians would quite naturally have found their way there). Then the party moves
forward again, this time by land. Christians from Rome
come out to meet Paul along the Appian Way, meeting him
at Appii Forum and the Three Taverns (see below).

This greeting greatly encourages Paul—perhaps he
realized now that his letter to the Romans had been a
success. Paul was not handed over to the authorities like

the other prisoners, but was allowed to live alone with a
soldier to guard him.

12. Syracuse
The beautiful modern harbour-city was already famous,
and had been so for centuries owing to the important Greek
colony there.

13. fetched a compass
This quaint phrase translates a Greek word *perielthontes,
having gone round*, and would mean that they had to make
a detour to get up to Rhegium owing to contrary winds.
But *perielthontes* is almost certainly a mistake for *periel-
ontes, having cast off*.

15. Appii forum and The three taverns
The first was a market town forty-three miles from Rome
along the Appian Way; the second a famous group of shops
or huts thirty-three miles on the same route. Some
Christians were faster travellers than others!

16. when we came to Rome
The last statement in the first person. Luke's path now
could not follow exactly that of Paul the prisoner.

the captain of the guard
This translates the Greek *stratopedarchos*, commander
of the Roman Emperor's bodyguard. But the whole phrase
rests on doubtful textual authority.

PAUL AND THE ROMAN JEWS
28.17-29

In Rome, although a nominal prisoner, Paul manages to
follow the same pattern as in all his missions—he first

approaches the Jews. They had to come to him, he could
not go to them. When he meets them, he gives a brief
summary of his case, explaining why he had been compelled
to appeal to Caesar, but hastily adding that he had not come
in any spirit of disloyalty to his own people. He claims, as
previously, to be a prisoner FOR THE HOPE OF ISRAEL. They
say that so far they have heard nothing against him, but
they have heard plenty against THIS SECT, i.e. Christianity.
They arrange for a larger gathering and Paul spends a whole
day expounding and testifying THE KINGDOM OF GOD, and
showing how the message of Jesus was in harmony with the
Law and the Prophets (cf. Jesus on the Emmaus journey,
Luke 24.25-27). It is interesting that the phrase ' kingdom
of God ' comes into prominence again in this final chapter.
There is the usual division of opinion (v. 24), and then Paul
makes a final solemn statement (25-27.) He uses words
which Jesus Himself had used (Luke 8.10), quoting from
Isaiah 6.9-10. The people of Israel hear, but do not understand, they see and do not perceive. This leads to yet one
more dramatic announcement that the gospel will be given
to the Gentiles (v. 28). BE IT KNOWN THEREFORE UNTO YOU,
THAT THE SALVATION OF GOD IS SENT UNTO THE GENTILES,
AND THAT THEY WILL HEAR IT. This is exactly the same
point of view as Paul expounds in Rom. 9–11. The natural
branches of the olive have been cut off through unbelief:
unnatural branches—the Gentiles—will now be grafted in.
Thus the great two-volume work of Luke-Acts ends as it
began by showing in unmistakable terms, that Christ's
gospel is ' a light to lighten the Gentiles '. Nothing can stop
the gospel—not even the perpetual unbelief of God's
ancient people. Like a chicken breaking the shell of its
enclosing egg, the power of Christ is such that it must burst
all barriers. New wine must be put into new bottles.

28. the salvation of God
    Cf. Luke 3.6.

UNHINDERED PREACHING
28.30-31

Acts closes with Paul living in his hired house, or—more probably—'at his own charges' two whole years, preaching and teaching 'without hindrance'. The very last word of the Greek text is *akōlutōs*, without obstacle. God's plan has succeeded. The gospel has reached 'the uttermost part of the earth', and there is boldly and effectively proclaimed. It is still the message of the Kingdom of God, but now is particularized in THOSE THINGS WHICH CONCERN THE LORD JESUS CHRIST.

There are one or two historical points about this ending of Acts. Why did Luke end his story where he did? (For this see Introduction, p. 21.) What happened at the end of the two years? Possibly the charge went by default. Possibly Paul was condemned and executed after his first trial. Possibly he was released, and subsequently re-arrested. Nobody knows. There is an unbroken tradition that Paul (with Peter) suffered martyrdom at Rome under Nero. Clement of Rome, writing in A.D. 96, says, 'Let us set before our eyes the good Apostles. . . . By reason of jealousy and strife Paul by his example pointed at the prize of patient endurance. After that he had been seven times in bonds, had been driven into Exile, had been stoned, had preached in the East and in the West, he won the noble renown which was the reward of his faith, having taught righteousness unto the whole world, and having reached the farthest bounds of the West; and when he had borne testimony before the rulers, so he departed from the world, and went unto the holy place, having been found a notable pattern of endurance.' These words *tend* to imply a mission to more westerly parts, e.g. Spain, and we know that Paul intended to evangelize there (see Rom. 15.24, 28). The Pastoral Epistles, whatever view we take of their authorship,

imply a further mission in the East after the end of Acts.
In the third century, Caius of Rome said that 'the trophies'
of those who founded the Church of Rome were to be seen
at the Vatican and on the Ostian Road. 'Trophies' were
shrines connected with the scene of deaths or burials. St.
Paul's is now covered by the great church of 'St. Paul without the walls', on the road from Rome to Ostia. That,
however, is a small part of his memorial. His real memorial
is European Christendom, and the world-wide Church which
has sprung from it.

A NOTE ON THE TEXT OF ACTS

One problem that arises with all ancient literature, which had to be copied and re-copied by hand, is that of discovering what were the actual words written by the original author. The study of this problem is called textual criticism. As far as most of the New Testament is concerned it may be said that while there is frequently much uncertainty as to the *exact* words used, the differences rarely amount to anything that would affect the general sense of any passage. There is, however, a special problem in Acts. The form of text thought by scholars to approximate most closely to the original is that followed by the Revised Version, which represents the text found in the so-called great Uncials, usually designated by the symbols *aleph* and B, and also supported by certain 'minuscule' manuscripts. These authorities frequently diverge from the text found in the Authorized Version, which follows a class of text known as the Byzantine, and which originated as a revision of the then known texts made early in the fourth century. They also diverge from the text of the great Cambridge manuscript known as Codex Bezae (D), which itself finds support in renderings in the Old Latin and Old Syriac versions. Now in Acts, the special readings of the D group (commonly called the 'Western' text) are particularly frequent. They usually expand the text of the old Uncials so that, in all, the D text is about ten per cent longer than the B text. This fact has led to much discussion as to the nature and authority of the D text. Some scholars (e.g. A. C. Clark— see bibliography) hold that the Western readings are in the main the accurate renderings of the original; some hold that Luke produced his work in two editions, one giving us

172

the 'Western' Acts, and one the B version. Both these views are now widely rejected, and the usual view is that the Western readings are of small importance as evidence for the original text of Acts. The 'Western' text is certainly very ancient, probably going back to the later second century, but most of the readings are expansions, paraphrases, and smoothings-out of a text very much like that of B. The D readings are of importance in other ways, e.g. in throwing light on contemporary theological tendencies. One of the most important Western readings (occurring as it happens in A.V., Acts 8.37) is the dialogue between Philip and the Ethiopian Eunuch, when he asked for baptism. 'And Philip said, If thou believest with all thine heart thou mayest. And he answered and said, I believe that Jesus Christ is the Son of God.' This is probably not original but very interesting as representing common Church practice at the time it arose. Another important reading in the Western text is the rendering of the Apostolic Decree at Acts 15.20 and 29. This omits the reference to 'things strangled', and adds the negative form of the Golden Rule. This is a revision of the earlier form, intended to present the decree as a general moral injunction rather than as a food law.

Students below University standard need not distress themselves by struggling with the complexities of the text of Acts. These notes are given to make intelligible the occasional references in the Commentary to the Western text.

APPENDIX

page 15, line 2   most modern scholars

The word 'most' is probably still justified from a purely numerical point of view. In view, however, of the retreat of some distinguished scholars from support of the Lucan authorship, it might be safer to say *many modern scholars*.

page 17, top paragraph

This is written on the assumption that Colossians was written by Paul. Early nineteenth century doubts on this matter have received some support from recent 'computer' analysis of New Testament documents, but careful scholars (e.g. Prof. C. F. D. Moule) are still ready to accept the Pauline authorship.

page 17, 4(a)

Details are available in Bruce, op. cit., p. 5 and B.C. III, p. 442.

pages 20-21

One difficulty that I did not point out in the earlier edition in accepting a very early date for *Luke-Acts* is that Luke is always assumed to have used *Mark* and *Mark* itself is usually dated about A.D. 65.

page 21

Prof. Bo Reicke, now of Basel University, has, in the book referred to in the enlarged Bibliography, given new support to the view often put forward earlier, that sections 2.42-4.31 and 4.32-5.42 are 'doublets', i.e. they represent two similar, but not identical, accounts of the same event.

page 24   Last paragraph before The Theme of Acts
I should not want seriously to vary the terms in which I
summed up the question of reliability ten years ago.   But it
should be said that recent writers (esp. Conzelmann and Haenchen) have laid great stress on the writer of Acts as 'a com-
poser'.   The more freedom the author claimed in the manipu-
lation of his material, or even, as they would think, in the
original composition of it, the less close is the link between
'what actually happened' and 'what is actually written'.   As
I have said elsewhere (essay, 'Church History in Acts: is it
reliable?', in *History and Chronology in the New Testament*,
S.P.C.K., 1965), 'We may believe that the book we have
springs from an encounter between a real writer of history—
probably Luke—and the real past, mediated to him by a number of traditions.'

page 25   Ten lines from foot of page: instructed
I have taken this word (from Luke 1. 4, *katēchēthēs*) in the
usual sense of 'been taught, been catechised'.   Perhaps an
alternative translation 'received hostile information against',
in accordance with the use in Acts 21.21, ought to be mentioned as a possible alternative.   The New English Bible
leaves both doors open with the phrase, 'about which you
have been informed'.

pages 26-27   A supernatural event in two stages
The interpretation I have given here, and on pp. 31-32,
sections 11 and 12, has received vigorous support from M. D.
Goulder in his book, noted in the Bibliography, *Type and
History in Acts*.   There (pp. 36-39) the author not only refers
approvingly to what is said in this Commentary, but devotes
much of his space to adducing detailed supporting evidence to
show that much or all of *Acts* was written in conscious imita-
tion of the story in *Luke*, or even in some cases *vice versa*.
Nothing written since 1953 makes the thesis laid down in the
Torch Commentary less worthy of serious examination.

page 33, line 11
Modern history moves so rapidly that even a decade alters
the 'missionary map' considerably.   Political developments in

the areas mentioned make it harder to see these continents as strong Christian centres for missionary propaganda. Acts, however, if it teaches nothing else, teaches us to look beyond the superficial and to see God at work, often in mysterious ways, as He carries forward His purpose.

page 41   End of Section 5

The list of peoples in 2.9-11 has continued to attract the ingenuity of scholars. Some associate it with the Signs of the Zodiac. Goulder claims that it stems from Gen. 10, and is built up on ' the grandsons of Noah ', who were thought to have peopled the earth. By various efforts of emendation the number of peoples involved has been trimmed to make 12 peoples, or $12+1$, where Judaea is considered to represent 12 tribes, and the remaining 12 peoples the Gentile world. Most of these schemes are too ingenious to prove convincing. In the scheme of Acts, Pentecost concerns the Jews, scattered throughout the world. The turn of the Gentiles is to come later.

page 48   End of section before The Immediate Challenge

While the thesis first made famous by Prof. C. H. Dodd has not yet been seriously shaken, those who stand for a late date for Acts (e.g. M. G. Goulder and J. C. O'Neill) have to find an explanation for the speeches *other* than that they represent the primitive message as it was actually preached. So they stress the way in which the speeches follow on, one after the other, each adapted to the stage in missionary strategy then reached. This leads them to see the speeches more than ever as free compositions of the author. O'Neill sees in the speeches the theology of salvation as understood by the Christian fathers of the second century. Though well argued, it is a thesis not likely to be rapidly or widely accepted. It involves us in regarding Clement of Rome (A.D. 96) and Ignatius (A.D. 110) as more primitive than Acts! Not many will be able to digest this unpalatable morsel of speculation!

page 54   Last line but one

Add: Some distinguished scholars (Prof. C. F. D. Moule, Prof. C. K. Barrett and Miss M. D. Hooker) have questioned whether there was any widespread use of Isaiah 53 and other servant passages by Jesus and his first followers. Others, like Prof. Jeremias, adhere to the general view taken in long paragraph on this page.

page 55   Note on v. 16

Add: The New English Bible renders it thus: 'And the name of Jesus, by awakening faith, has strengthened this man, whom ye see and know, and this faith has made him completely well, as you can all see for yourselves.'

page 59   V. 28

Statements similar to that in this note are very frequently made, but I should now want to emphasize that Luke's *Gospel* must always be kept in mind when considering the theological standpoint of *Acts*. Even if there is some stress in the Gospel of the humanity of Christ in his sympathy and suffering, it is also quite clear that His death—described at great length—is the means whereby He fulfilled the promise that He would be the Saviour of His people (see Luke 1.68, 77; 2.11, 29; 23.34—if text is correct here; and especially 24.46-7).

page 62   Under A Wave of Healing Miracles, last sentence

Perhaps it would be safer to say: 'it shows how pre-eminent Peter's position as the leader of the apostolic band was in the mind of the writer of Acts'.

pages 66-67   Hellenists and Hebrews

In the past we have tended to speak of these two groups as though they comprised the two principal divisions of the Jewish people. This is probably still basically true, but the discoveries concerning the Qumran community (known through the Dead Sea Scrolls) have directed attention to heretical or schismatic elements among the Jews and it may be that different elements in the Jewish Christian Church reflected different groups in Judaism, from which they had been recruited.

page 78   Foot of page, on v. 5
The ruins of the Herodian city, Sebaste, situated on a lofty hill with extensive views, show what a flourishing capital it was at the time of the first Christian mission there.

page 86   V. 18
It should be noted that in the three verses, 17, 18 and 19, we have a whole network of ideas that came to be important in the sacramental life of the Early Church: illumination (sight after blindness), one of the early names for baptism; baptism itself; laying on of hands; the gift of the Holy Ghost; the taking of food. It is a matter of judgment how far the writer had these ecclesiastical concepts in his mind, or whether we have here the kind of raw material out of which the later church patterns developed.

page 89   V. 32
Now the site of the Tel Aviv airport!

page 90   V. 36, Joppa
Now Jaffa, just visible southwards from Tel Aviv.

page 91   On 10.1 Caesarea
Extensive excavations have laid bare much of this important sea-port and administrative capital.

page 93, top
Many scholars still write in this way, but Dr Alan Richardson in his Bampton Lectures, *History, Sacred and Profane,* takes the view that the Resurrection *should* be thought of as taking place within the course of human history, and needing to be estimated from the 'disturbance' it caused within the field of historical events.

page 125, line 24
Even now, to stand on Areopagus (Mars Hill) and to look across to the great hill crowned by the Parthenon, and all around to the many other fine buildings, makes the modern traveller realize what faith and courage it must have taken to confront ancient Athens with the simple gospel of salvation through Christ crucified.

page 128   End of third para. (after ' One, Living and Eternal, God')

Recent commentators (especially Haenchen) stress the point that in the speech of Paul at Athens, Luke is giving a model of the kind of preaching that was needed to attract Gentiles, who had not come under the influence of the Old Testament. For such hearers, ' their own poets ' had to take the place of the Old Testament. The problem of the right starting-point confronts every ' missionary ' preacher, whether in nominally Christian, or in non-Christian lands.

page 129   V. 22

Haenchen points out that the phrase ' in the midst of Mars Hill ' (Areopagus) lends weight to the view that *the place*—the rocky eminence still visible in Athens—rather than the assembly is intended. Cf. original note on v. 19.

page 135, lines 11-12

The example from Paul's baptism is not quite relevant, for there *was* a laying-on-of-hands in his case (see extra note provided for 9.17-19, p. 178) though on that occasion it *preceded* baptism, and was connected with Paul's recovery from blindness.

page 144, line 11

' he ' means Luke, not Paul.

page 145   On v. 16, Mnason

Since writing the first edition, I have become even more interested in the parallels between Luke and Acts, particularly in the two ' Passion narratives '. I was examining the possible parallel between Simon of Cyrene (Luke 23.26) and Mnason of Cyprus (Acts 21.16) as two men who in some way assisted Jesus and Paul respectively, when I noticed that as used in the Greek, the two words are *almost* anagrams, SIMONA (acc.) and MNASONI (dative). I do not know whether this has ever been noticed before!

pages 148-149

Recent scholarship insists that Paul was a thorough Hellenist and is less willing to accept the picture given in Acts of Paul as being brought up in Jerusalem.